Jesus
or
the Church?

By: Anthony Roberts

Copyright 2023 Anthony Roberts

All rights reserved. No part of this publication may be reproduced, distributed, or transmitted in any form or by any means, including photocopying, recording, or other electronic or mechanical methods, without the prior written permission of the publisher, except in the case of brief quotations embodied in critical reviews and certain other noncommercial uses permitted by copyright law.

This book is dedicated to those who verify all things before following them. They seek the truth, and once they have found it, they have the will and the courage to free themselves from deep-rooted preconceptions.

Table of Contents

Chapter 1: Introduction 2

Chapter 2: History of Christianity 4

Chapter 3: Is Jesus God? 7

Chapter 4: The God Incarnate doctrine 13

Chapter 5: The Crucifixion 21

Chapter 6: The Trinity 24

Chapter 7: The Atonement and the Original Sin 32

Chapter 8: Paul, the 'Corrupter of Christianity' 39

Chapter 9: Commentary on frequently quoted verses 44

Chapter 10: The 'Get out of jail card' 68

Chapter 11: Conclusion 81

Chapter 12: Glossary 86

Chapter 1
Introduction

What is the definition of a Christian? Is he simply the one who goes to Church, or is he the one who follows the teachings of Jesus Christ? On the surface, it may seem that the two are the same. However, with a closer look at the Bible, and also the history of Christianity, it becomes evident that there is a marked difference between the two.

It is not uncommon to find many Christians who have never read the Bible even once, let alone the history of Christianity. If any time is given, it is spent by going to Church once in a while and listening to the local Pastor/Priest, but never questioning or investigating the truth of what is being said. Various doctrines, that are taken for granted, are never looked into to verify whether they are supported by Biblical references or not. Since this research will contain numerous Biblical references, it is important first to establish two matters:

1- For a non-Christian reader, Biblical verses do not constitute absolute truth nor are they considered the Word of God. However, Biblical verses are quoted in this book because the target readers are primarily Christians who may wish to investigate the origin of various doctrines advocated by the Church and which are fundamental to Christianity.

2- The second important issue is whether some Biblical verses should be taken literally or allegorically. It has been known in various debates that one side regards the verses that agree with their claims as literal while they describe the verses that contradict their claims as being allegorical. This may be convenient for some but it is invariably a distortion of the truth.

One such example is when the words, "My Father is greater than I" (John 14:28) are quoted to the believers in the Trinity. These words contradict the heart of the Trinity which has Jesus and God as equal.

When presented with this verse, the advocates of the Trinity are known to say, "Oh, but this verse is allegorical" or "You are taking this verse out of context", but when they are told, "Then should we also take the phrase of Son of God as allegorical"? They quickly reply "No, that is literal."

For that reason, and unless there exists clear justification, all Biblical verses employed in this book will be regarded as literal, and to be taken for their straightforward meaning.

Chapter 2
History of Christianity

If we start by looking into Christianity as a religion, when it was established and by whom, we discover some startling facts. All the first believers and followers of Jesus were Jews. Jesus himself lived all his life as a Jew. All the first followers of Jesus, and for the first 200 years, prayed in the Synagogues. The earliest known Church was not built until two whole centuries after the death of Jesus. That Church was built in the year 232 A. D. and is found at Dura-Euphrates (The History of Christianity, a Lion Handbook, p. 76).

Up until the death of Jesus, Christianity as a religion independent from Judaism, did not exist. In his own words, Jesus asserted that he did not come to establish a new religion, but that he had come to fulfil the prophecies in the Torah:

"Think not that I am come to destroy the law, I am not come to destroy, but to fulfil." (Matthew 5:17-18)

Many doctrines that constitute the foundation of Christianity, such as the Trinity, have no origin in the Bible. The article of faith up until the end of the 2nd century was:

"I believe in God the Almighty." (Articles of the Apostolic Creed, Theodore Zahn, p. 33-37)

Between 180 and 210 A. D. the word Father was added before the Almighty. This was opposed by a number of bishops. Bishops Victor and Zephysius immediately defied this addition stating that it is a sin to add or subtract from the Scripture. In addition, in those early years, the Holy Spirit was still understood to mean a superior angel, not of one substance with God.

Arius, a senior presbyter, was among the many who believed that the Father alone was God and that the Son did not possess by nature or right any of the divine qualities of immortality, sovereignty and purity.

With the aid of reason, Arius proceeded to prove that Jesus was not God. Arius started from the following verse:

"For God so loved the world, that He gave his only begotten Son, that whosoever believeth in him should not perish, but have everlasting life." (John 3:16)

Arius argued that since Jesus was "begotten", then there was a time when Jesus did not exist. Therefore Jesus is not eternal, and since God is eternal, Jesus cannot be God (The History of Christianity, a Lion Handbook, p. 164). Arius also stated his case with evidence from the Scripture. If Jesus said the following:

"My Father is greater than I." (John 14:28)

"No messenger is greater than the One who sent him." (John 13:16)

then to believe that God and Jesus are equal is to deny the truth of the Scripture.

It was not until the Council of Nicaea in 325 A. D., and against strong opposition from many bishops, that the concept of the Trinity was adopted. To exclude the arguments of Arius the council produced its own creed, which was called the Creed of Nicaea.

The Creed of Nicaea

> We believe in one God the Father, Almighty, maker of all things visible and invisible; and in one Lord Jesus Christ, the Son of God, begotten of the Father, only-begotten that is, from the substance of the Father; God from God, light from light, Very God from Very God (The History of Christianity, a Lion Handbook, p. 177).

Once this creed was approved and set as law, the cast was set and the corruption was born. The council also dictated that all gospels not in agreement with the creed should be burned. It became a capital offence to possess an unauthorised gospel. What ensued was that over a million Christians were killed in the years that followed.

The Creed of Nicaea, which was an evident encroachment on the Scripture, ultimately failed to answer the following questions:

1- If Jesus is made of the same <u>substance</u> as God, as the creed states, he must be a god as well; and if he is a god, is he a different god? If he is, that would make them two gods, but the creed says: "We believe in <u>one</u> God."

2- If Jesus is a god but not a different god then he must be God himself. If that is the case, then how can God be "<u>begotten</u>"? A "begotten" god contradicts the concept of the Eternal God. Both of the above cases are in direct contradiction to the Bible. The first of these two possibilities, which makes Jesus a different god from God contradicts the Bible which asserts that God is One and indivisible:

"The first of all the commandments is Hear, O Israel, the Lord our God is One." (Mark 12:29)

The second possibility is that there is only one god who came down to earth in the form of a man. If that is so, and since God is indivisible, then we must conclude that God and Jesus must be one being. However, this does not conform with many verses in the Bible where Jesus and God are clearly spoken of as two separate beings, nor the verses where Jesus speaks to God and addresses God as "You."

Chapter 3
Is Jesus God?

In this chapter, 12 Biblical references are presented to address the all-important question of whether Jesus is God:

1- If God came down to earth as a man, one would expect that after the end of His life on earth, and upon His return to Heaven, He would be fully God. This is not in agreement with the following verse:

"So then after the Lord had spoken unto them, he was received up into Heaven, and sat on the right hand of God." (Mark 16:19)

This verse completely invalidates the claim that during his life on earth, Jesus was fully man but after his resurrection, he became fully God. If that is so, how can Jesus after resurrection, as fully God, be sitting "on the right hand of God"?

This verse, which speaks about Jesus after he was raised up into Heaven, clearly indicates that God and Jesus are not one being and that Jesus is not God, not on earth and not in heaven.

2- In numerous verses, we read about Jesus praying to God, such as:

"He often withdrew into the wilderness and prayed." (Luke 5:16)

"And when he had sent the multitudes away, he went up on a mountain by himself to pray." (Matthew 14:23)

"And being in anguish he prayed more earnestly: and his sweat was as it were great drops of blood falling down to the ground." (Luke 22:44)

These verses are of great significance. How can Jesus be God if he was praying to God? Who was Jesus praying to? Would God pray and implore Himself?

When faced with such a dilemma, the Clergy have been known to label the above verses as allegorical. At other times, they suggest that Jesus was only praying symbolically to teach the people how to conduct prayer. This argument is clearly invalid for the simple reason that the words "wilderness" in Luke 5:16, and the words "by himself" in Matthew 14:23 indicate that at those specific times, Jesus was all on his own while praying. He could not have been teaching anyone then.

3- "He walked away, perhaps a stone's throw, and knelt down and prayed this prayer: 'Father, if you are willing, please take away this cup of horror from me. But <u>I want Your will, not mine.</u>'" (Luke 22:41-42)

If Jesus and God are one God, how can God have two different wills?

4- "I do nothing on my own authority." (John 8:28)

"I do as the Father has <u>commanded me</u>." (John 14:31)

Is it possible for one God to command himself?

5- "Jesus lifted up his eyes and said, 'Father, <u>I thank thee that Thou hast heard me</u>. And I knew that Thou always hears me: but because of the people which stand by I said it, that they may believe that Thou hast sent me.'" (John 11:41-42)

If Jesus is God, is it possible for God not to hear Himself? Is there a need for God to thank Himself for hearing Himself?

6- "And Jesus … for forty days in the wilderness was tempted by the devil." (Luke 4:1-2)

We also read in the Bible the following:

"God cannot be tempted by the devil." (James 1:13)

If God cannot be tempted by the devil, and Jesus was tempted by the devil, how can Jesus be God?

7- Jesus himself refused to be called Son of God on a number of occasions. In the following verse, he rebukes the ones who called him Son of God, preferring the title of Messiah:

"And devils came out of many, crying out and saying, 'You are the Son of God!' And he, rebuking them, did not allow them to speak, for they knew that he was the Messiah." (Luke 4:41)

The refusal of Jesus to be called the Son of God and choosing instead the title of Son of Man also occurred during the trial at the Sanhedrin. When he was asked if he claimed to be the Son of God, he affirmed that he was the Son of Man:

"Then the high priest stood up and said to Jesus, 'Are you not going to answer? What is this testimony that these men are bringing against you?' But Jesus remained silent.

The high priest said to him, 'I charge you under oath by the living God: Tell us if you are the Messiah, the Son of God.'

So you say. But I tell you this: from now you shall see the Son of Man seated at the right hand of God." (Matthew 26:62-64)

8- On numerous occasions Jesus speaks of himself as a prophet:

"A prophet is not without honour except in his home town and his own house." (Matthew 13:57) (Mark 6:4) and (Luke 4:24)

We also read:

"I must journey today, tomorrow and the day following for it cannot be that a prophet should perish outside of Jerusalem." (Luke 13:33)

"This is the prophet Jesus." (Matthew 21:11)

"He who receives a prophet in the name of a prophet shall receive a prophet's reward. And he who receives a righteous man in the name of a righteous man shall receive a righteous man's reward." (Matthew 10:41)

9- Jesus also spoke of himself as the messenger of God:

"No messenger is greater than the One who sent him." (John 13:16)

The distinction in this verse is made very clear by Jesus between himself and the One who sent him. This is again made clear in the following verse:

"And this is eternal life, that they may know You, the only true God, and Jesus Christ whom You have sent." (John 17:3)

These verses clearly speak of two separate beings. To claim that Jesus and God are one reduces these verses to mere nonsense. In addition, how can Jesus be God when he addresses God as the only true God? He also stated that the only true God had sent him.

10- In various other verses Jesus is referred to as the servant of God:

"Here is My servant whom I have chosen." (Matthew 12:18)

"To you first, God having raised up His servant Jesus, sent him to bless you." (Acts 3:26)

These two verses in the New Testament are regarded to be the fulfilment of the following prophecy in the Old Testament:

"Here is my servant, whom I uphold, my chosen one in whom I delight; I will put my Spirit on him, and he will bring justice to the nations." (Isaiah 42:1)

The words in the Old Testament as well as the New Testament speak of Jesus as the servant of God and not as God.

Once again, the Clergy will argue that the term "servant" in those verses is allegorical and should not be taken literally; the usual escape card.

The truth of the matter is that all the verses that speak of Jesus as a prophet of God, a messenger of God and indeed the servant of God affirm the fact that Jesus was a man who worshipped God like any other mortal.

11- Jesus did not think of himself as being perfect, let alone divine. He knew in his heart that only God is perfect:

"Why do you call me good? No one is good but One, that is God." (Mark 10:18)

These are hardly the words of someone who thought of himself as God come down to earth in the form of a man. In fact, in these words, Jesus makes a very clear distinction between God and himself.

12- In all the Bible there is not one verse where Jesus says that he is God come down to earth, that he is divine or that he should be worshipped. On the contrary, he taught the people to worship God in Heaven:

"You shall worship the Lord your God, and Him only you shall serve." (Luke 4:8)

Was Jesus God come down to earth and did not know it himself? The divinity of Jesus is never taught by Jesus and has no origin in the Bible but was adopted sometime after the death of Jesus.

In addition to the previous evidence from the New Testament that refutes the divinity of Jesus, it can also be demonstrated that Jesus' divinity is inconsistent with the prophecies contained in the Old Testament about the coming of the Messiah.

Jesus was a Jew who lived and worshipped God according to the law given to Moses. Jesus himself said:

"Think not that I am come to destroy the law, I am not come to destroy, but to fulfil." (Matthew 5:17-18)

With the words "to fulfil" Jesus was referring to the prophecies in the Jewish Scripture. These prophecies speak about the coming of the Messiah, the King of Jews. We do not find one prophecy that speaks of the coming of God in the form of a man or of a divine Son of God. All the prophecies spoke of the coming of the King of Jews not of God.

Chapter 4
The God Incarnate doctrine

The concept of God coming down to earth in the form of a man God Incarnate, has probably been accepted by most Christians because a visual representation of God is easier to connect with than an abstract God that can never be seen. To think of God in a human form is at least something to cling to.

The concept of God Incarnate, compassionate as it may seem on the surface, is philosophically inconsistent with the divine plan for the following reasons:

1- The concept of God Incarnate is irrational in the sense that it channels man's approach to God through the physical form rather than by escape from it. The purpose of any revelation is to inspire man to elevate his soul to seek nearness to God, rather than for God to descend to a physical form to convince man.

2- It does not seem just or fair that God should send messengers to all communities and nations except one particular people to whom He should go to them in person. We are always made to believe that God loves all mankind equally. Why would God grant one people such a great blessing that is not given to others?

3- The divine plan entails the sending of messengers across the ages to deliver guidance to mankind. For God to substitute the sending of messengers with coming down in person would seem like a change of plan on God's side. It is not becoming of the Omnipotent God to adapt to accommodate man.

4- The concept of God coming down to earth and taking such great suffering upon Himself defies the definition of an Omnipotent God. Furthermore, to suggest that God subjected Himself to all that suffering because He so much loved man is even more sacrilege. It is disrespectful of the Majesty and Exalted nature of God. In addition, God's love for man cannot be increased by having to suffer Himself. This masochistic scenario is unfit and insulting to the Almighty God. Instead, God's love is expressed through His mercy, compassion and forgiveness.

As an example, a loving father who wishes to forgive his misbehaving children does not love his children any more by saying, "I love you so much my children, I wish to forgive you so I will beat myself up."

5- The concept of God Incarnate is self-contradictory because the person of the incarnate Jesus is credited with possessing two sets of attributes which sharply contradict one another. It was Plato who first stressed the difference between earthly and heavenly worlds. The former is changeable, imperfect and finite, while the latter is unchangeable, perfect and infinite. Later, the same contrasts were applied to man and God (The Debate about Christ, Don Cuppit, p. 25).

According to the God Incarnate doctrine, Jesus was called upon to unite the two polarities. As God, he was infinite, perfect and all-powerful; but as man, he was finite, imperfect, weak and afflicted. Since he was one person and not two, he was meant to be simultaneously infinite and finite, incapable of temptation and capable of temptation, perfect and imperfect and so on. If such claims are self-contradictory then the doctrine of God Incarnate cannot be true. It is nonsense.

6- The God Incarnate doctrine, which is interlocked with the concept of salvation attainable only through belief in Jesus Christ, is also erroneous because it automatically means that damnation awaits all those who were unfortunate to have lived before the time of Jesus. Such people never knew Jesus to believe in him. In divine terms that would seem unjust.

7- The God Incarnate doctrine is also in contradiction with the following verse:

"No man shall see Me and live." (Exodus 33:20)

If God came down to earth, albeit in the form of a man, and was seen and touched by man then the previous verse would be meaningless.

8- The God Incarnate doctrine also raises serious questions concerning the absolute ability of God. God, being perfection, does not fail in any endeavour that He undertakes. He only needs to say "be" and it is. Now to say that Jesus was God coming down to earth to deliver mankind from sin and convert the sinners to righteous believers, we would immediately be faced with another dilemma. No one can dispute the holy message delivered by Jesus, his great impact on humanity, nor the divine revelation he delivered from God. However, the fact still remains that there was a huge number of people who rejected Jesus and the message he delivered at that time. This continued across the generations and today there are millions upon millions who are not only non-believers but who are committing all kinds of blasphemy and great sins. Would that mean that God failed in His mission of coming down to deliver the sinners to righteous believers?

The sense in which God is called free differs from the sense in which man is called free as Don Cupitt wrote (The Debate about Christ, Don Cuppit, p. 19). God is called free in the sense that His purpose cannot fail. His will is at no time confined, dependent or challenged. If God says, "I will become incarnate and save men," then nothing can stop it from happening. Failure in any form or degree is inconsistent with the concept of the Omnipotent God.

To support the claim that Jesus was God coming down to earth, or that Jesus was the Son of God, the advocates employ the following arguments:

1- Jesus was blessed with the Holy Spirit

2- The virgin birth

3- The nature of his miracles

<u>Jesus blessed with the Holy Spirit</u>

Indeed the Bible affirms that Jesus was blessed with the Holy Spirit. However, a careful study of the Bible confirms that Jesus was not the only one blessed with the Holy Spirit. The Bible speaks of others who were also blessed with the Holy Spirit. The following verse speaks about John the Baptist:

"He will also be filled with the Holy Spirit." (Luke 1:15)

We are told the same about John's father, the righteous priest Zacharias. He too was "filled with the Holy Spirit." (Luke 1:67)

It is a good idea to pause here and inquire into the real meaning of the Holy Spirit. As mentioned earlier, we have seen that for the first two hundred years after the death of Jesus, when the concept of the Trinity was not yet adopted, the Holy Spirit was still understood to mean a superior angel, not of one substance with God. This definition is supported by several verses in the Bible. The following verses assert that meaning:

"Now the birth of Jesus Christ was as follows: After his mother Mary was betrothed to Joseph, and before they came together, she was found with child of the Holy Spirit." (Matthew 1:18)

16

Now consider the following verse:

"Now in the sixth month, the angel Gabriel was sent by God to a city of Galilee called Nazareth, to a virgin betrothed to a man called Joseph of the house of David. The virgin's name was Mary." (Luke 1:26-27)

From these verses, we see that the Holy Spirit and Gabriel are used interchangeably.

Thus to say that someone was blessed with the Holy Spirit is to say that God supported him with the angel Gabriel to be his guardian.

<u>The Virgin Birth</u>

The Church has used the Virgin Birth strongly to favour the Son of God concept. The claim is that since Jesus had no human father, his father must be God in Heaven. Jesus is, therefore, the true Son of God. The simple argument against that is put forward by referring to Adam. According to Genesis, Adam did not have a father or a mother. Should not Adam also be the Son of God? And if he is indeed called the Son of God as in, "Adam the <u>Son of God</u>." (Luke 3:38), shouldn't all the seed of Adam be called children of God? And if that is indeed the case, should we still insist that Jesus was the only Son of God?

"We are the <u>children of God</u>." (Romans 8:16)

"You are the <u>sons of the living God</u>." (Hosea 1:10)

"Blessed are the peacemakers for they shall be called <u>sons of God</u>." (Matthew 5:9)

"Those who are led by God's spirit are <u>God's sons</u>." (Romans 8:14)

Should the Church still insist on denying that Jesus taught that all people are children of God? And if Jesus indeed said just that as in:

"I ascend to <u>my Father</u> and <u>your Father</u>, to <u>my God and your God</u>." (John 20:17)

Should we still insist on the narrow sense of Jesus being the only Son of God?

The Miracles of Jesus

The awesome nature of the miracles performed by Jesus, not the least the raising of the dead, was also used to support the divinity of Jesus. However, the Bible testifies that all the miracles performed by Jesus were also performed by other prophets such as Elisha and Elijah, yet no one argues that these men are thus divine.

1- Feeding thousands with scarce food

The prophet Elisha fed great crowds with twenty barley loaves:

"42 A man from Baal-shalishah came to the man of God with his sack full of[a] twenty loaves of barley bread from the first bread of the harvest. Elisha said, "Give it to the people to eat."

43 But Elisha's attendant asked, "What? Am I to set this before a hundred men?"

"Give it to the people to eat," Elisha said, "for this is what the LORD says: 'They will eat, and they will have some leftover.'" 44 So he set it before them, and as the LORD had promised, they ate and had some leftover." (II Kings 4:42-44)

A similar event is found in (I Kings 17:14-16)

2- Healing leprosy

Elisha told Namaan, who was a leper, to wash in the Jordan River to be healed:

"Then went he (Namaan) down, and dipped himself seven times in the Jordan, according to the saying of the man of God; and his flesh was restored like the flesh of a little child." (II Kings 5:14)

3- Giving sight to the blind

"And Elisha prayed and said, 'Lord I pray Thee, open his eyes that he may see.' And the Lord opened the eyes of the young man, and he saw." (II Kings 6:17)

Some may argue that Elisha prayed for the young man to regain his sight, to which God opened his eyes, whereas Jesus himself returned the sight of the boy. This claim is debunked by the following words of Jesus in which he states that it is never he who does the miracles but God:

"I do nothing on my own authority." (John 8:28)

4- Raising the dead

Even this most awesome of miracles was performed by other prophets as the Bible testifies:

"And the Lord heard the voice of Elijah, and the soul of the child came back to him, and he recovered." (I Kings 17:22). Other similar events are in (II Kings 4:34) and (II Kings 13:21)

As mentioned, Jesus admitted on numerous occasions that whatever power he had was given to him by God:

"I do nothing on my own authority." (John 8:28)

"I do as the Father has commanded me." (John 14:31)

It is quite clear from these verses that Jesus is not speaking about himself. Clearly, he is speaking about the Almighty God whom he worships.

Besides acknowledging God's authority, and after performing such miracles, Jesus often prayed and thanked God for giving him such powers. In John's gospel, and after raising Lazarus, Jesus said:

"Father I thank You that You have heard me, and I know that You always hear me." (John 11:41-42)

If Jesus is God, who was he thanking?

These few verses indicate that it was God's authority that allowed such miracles. God grants these powers to his chosen prophets as a sign with which their people can identify and believe in them, not for their own people to turn them into gods.

Chapter 5
The Crucifixion

The Crucifixion of Jesus has been the subject of vast research. Was Jesus put on the cross? Did Jesus die on the cross? Such focal questions constitute the core of such research. The traditional Christian view is that Jesus was crucified and died on the cross to take away the sins of all mankind:

"For Christ's love compels us, because we are convinced that one died for all, and therefore all died. And he died for all, that those who live should no longer live for themselves but for him who died for them and was raised again." (2 Corinthians 5:14-15)

Although the Bible provides sufficient evidence to suggest that Jesus was indeed put on the cross, we also find strong evidence to indicate that he did not die on the cross. We read in the Bible that upon his arrest, or just before, Jesus went into deep prayers to God to save him from death:

"In the days of his earthly life, he offered up prayers, with loud cries and tears to God who was able to save him from death." (Hebrews 5:7)

This very significant verse indicates that upon hearing the prayers of Jesus, God has saved him from death. In other words, Jesus did not die on the cross. The Church may argue that the prayers of Jesus took place when he was in the grave and before being resurrected. However, this interpretation contradicts the words "In the days of his earthly life" which confirm that Jesus' prayer was while he was alive on earth and not dead in the grave. The same conclusion can be reached from the famous prophecy in Psalms:

"My God, my God, why have Thou forsaken me?" (Psalms 22:1)

"But you, Lord, do not be far from me. You are my strength; come quickly to help me." (Psalms 22:19)

The last words in Psalms 22 say:

"They shall come and shall declare His righteousness unto a people that shall be born, that He hath done it." (Psalms 22:31)

The words "He hath done it" once again indicate that God saved Jesus from death. Other verses seem to suggest that God had raised the soul of Jesus sometime before the crucifixion and that the one that was crucified by the Romans was no more than a living but soulless body (similar to the body of one who goes into a coma before dying). This view which shows God's immense compassion is strengthened by the following verse:

"But you, O Lord be merciful to me, and <u>raise me up</u>, that I may repay them ... my enemy <u>does not triumph over me</u>." (Psalms 41:10-11)

The words "<u>raise me up</u>" so that "<u>my enemy does not triumph over me</u>" also support the theory of the raising of the soul of Jesus before his enemy triumphs over him (before being crucified).

Further evidence to support this theory was discovered in 1945 when an Egyptian farmer digging for fertile soil near the village of Nag Hammadi unearthed a red clay jar. It contained thirteen papyrus scrolls which contained the now famous Gospel of Thomas.

The importance of this gospel is that it escaped the censorship and revision of the Roman orthodoxy. In the following extract, Jesus speaks in the first person:

"I did not succumb to them as they had planned ... and I did not die in reality but in appearance, lest I be put to shame by them." (The Holy Blood and the Holy Grail, Baigent, Leigh and Lincoln p. 403)

The words *"I did not die in reality"* support the belief that the soul of Jesus was raised before he was put on the cross.

Further support for this theory is found in the Gospel of St. Barnabas. Unlike the four better-known gospels (Mathew, Mark, Luke and John), the Gospel of St. Barnabas was written by a man who lived during the life of Jesus.

The Gospel of St. Barnabas also supports the theory that Jesus did not die on the cross. However, it presents a different scenario. According to his gospel, a process of substitution took place whereby Judas was transformed by God to look identical to Jesus and thus it was Judas who was arrested by the Romans and crucified.

In 1907 an English translation of the gospel of Barnabas was published by the Oxford University Press. Nearly the whole edition of this translation mysteriously disappeared from the market. Only two copies of this translation are known to exist today, one in the British Museum and the other in the Library of Congress in Washington.

The Gospel of St. Barnabas is discredited by Christian theologians and also by the Church even though Barnabas is referred to as an apostle by the early Christian Church (Acts 14:14). Barnabas is also praised in the Bible:

"Barnabas was a good man, full of the Holy Spirit and faith." (Acts 11:24)

Finally, it is important to distinguish between the term raising and the term resurrection. While the raising of Jesus would have happened to him while he was still alive and thus saved him from death, we find that the resurrection could not have occurred unless Jesus had died first. Given all the verses that speak of the raising and also being saved from death, the evidence seems to support the raising of a living Jesus by God to save him from death.

Chapter 6
The Trinity

The doctrine of the Trinity does not exist in the Bible and was never taught by Jesus. With this in mind, it is quite incredible that such a concept should become the foundation of faith upon which Christianity is based.

According to the Trinitarian scholars, the Trinity is a mystery that cannot be understood due to the inadequacy of our minds to comprehend it. It must therefore be accepted on faith and that is that.

It would make no sense therefore to argue or debate with those who state openly that they do not understand what they are preaching. Rather than debate them, it can be shown how the Trinity doctrine violates the Bible.

If we first look at the Hebrew Bible (the Old Testament), we find numerous unquestionable verses that assert that God is "One" God. Such verses (below) make the attempts of those who endeavor to prove a plurality of persons in God, which is a most enigmatic concept, futile and without Scriptural support:

- "Hear, O Israel, The Lord our God, the Lord is one." (Deuteronomy 6:4)

- "You shall have no other Gods before me." (Exodus 20:3)

- "See now that I myself am He, there is no God besides me." (Deuteronomy 32:39)

- "To whom will you compare Me? Or who is My equal?" (Isaiah 40:25)

- "I am the first and I am the last, apart from Me there is no God." (Isaiah 44:6)

- "Is there any God besides me?" (Isaiah 44:8)

- "There is no God apart from me; a just God, and a Saviour: there is none but me." (Isaiah 45:21)

- "I am God, and there is no other; I am God, and there is none like me." (Isaiah 46:9)

- "Let them know You, whose name is the Lord, that You alone are the Most High over all the earth." (Psalms 83:18)

- "For You are great and do marvelous deeds; You alone are God." (Psalms 86:10)

It is apparent from the verses above that God has always been represented as "One" person or being.

When we look at the New Testament, we find that there is mention of the Father, the Son and the Holy Spirit as in the King James Bible which was authorised in 1611:

"For there are three that bear witness in Heaven, the Father, the Word and the Holy Spirit and those three are one. And there are three that bear witness on earth; the Spirit the water and the blood, and these three agree as one." (1 John 5:7-8)

However, the following sentence: "For there are three that bear witness in Heaven, the Father, the Word and the Holy Spirit and those three are one" has been expunged in the Revised Standard Version of 1952 and 1971 and also in many other Bibles as it was an addition that had encroached on the original Greek text.

The following list shows some examples of Bibles in which the above sentence does not exist:

- American Standard Version - Christian Standard Bible - Common English Bible - Disciples' Literal New Testament - English Standard Version - Expanded Bible - Good News Translation - New American

Bible - New English Translation - New Living Translation - New Revised Standard Version - Revised Standard Version - World English Bible

None of the Bibles in the list above have the words "those three are one."

In addition, none of the Bibles in the list have the sentence, "the Father, the Word and the Holy Spirit."

The common translation is:

"For there are three who testify the Spirit, the water, and the blood; and the three are in agreement."

Furthermore, the Trinity offers a most irrational situation when it speaks of the Father as Creator, the Son as Redeemer and the Spirit as Sanctifier. This irrational arrangement will have us believe that God is a committee of three with distinct divided functions. This is in clear contradiction to the concept of the One Indivisible God whose authority encompasses all things.

The frequency with which God is called "the Father" is extensive. In the New Testament, God is called "the Father" in no less than 122 passages. In contrast, we do not see even one verse where the phrase "God the Son" is mentioned.

Still in the Bible, we read the words of Jesus that confirm that God is the only God and that he was only sent by God:

"How can you believe, when you receive glory from one another and do not seek the glory that comes from the only God?" (John 5:44)

"And this is eternal life, that they may know You, the only true God, and Jesus Christ whom You have sent." (John 17:3)

Unlike the Trinity doctrine which speaks of Jesus as God, the above words are a clear declaration from Jesus that he is not God, but that he was sent by the "only true God."

The concept of the Trinity was formulated by Athanasius - an Egyptian deacon from Alexandria (The History of Christianity, a Lion Handbook, p. 172-177). This was accepted by the Council of Nicaea in 325 A. D. which was held three centuries after the death of Jesus. No doubt Roman Paganism had an influence on this doctrine (the Triune God). Around the same time, new doctrines were introduced while various existing ones were modified.

The Saturday Sabbath of the Jews was shifted to Sunday. The birth of the sun god Mithra, December 25th, was adopted as Jesus' birthday. Many Pagan customs were Christianised, for example, the use of candles, incense and garlands. These customs were opposed by the early Church because they symbolised paganism, however, these have become commonplace today.

Some other pagan customs that were also Christianised are in clear violation of the Bible. One such custom is the cutting down and decorating of trees for Christmas. On that subject, the Bible says:

"For the customs of the people are in vain; for one cutteth a tree from the forest ... they decorate it with silver and gold." (Jeremiah 10:2-5)

The above are some of the concepts and customs introduced after the death of Jesus, mostly from Roman paganism, and which have no origin in the Bible.

One additional problematic consequence of the Trinity arises when we revisit the following two verses:

"We are the <u>children of God</u>." (Romans 8:16)

"You are the <u>sons of the living God</u>." (Hosea 1:10)

The problem with the Trinity in the light of these two verses is connected to what is called Syllogism. Syllogism is a form of rational reasoning whereby we have two given propositions called the premises, then together they lead to a valid and rational conclusion.

27

<u>Example:</u>

1- All men are mortal (premise)

2- Caesar is a man (premise)

therefore:

3- Caesar is mortal (conclusion)

With regards to the Trinity, the premises are as follows:

1- We are children and sons of God (Romans 8:16)

2- Jesus is God (Trinity doctrine)

The rational and valid conclusion that emerges from those two premises is: We are children and sons of Jesus.

But since we are not children and sons of Jesus, then one of the two premises above is incorrect and must be rejected. The question is: Should we reject the two Biblical verses above or should we reject the concept of the Trinity; a concept and a word that are found nowhere in the Bible?

<u>Was the Trinity a political solution?</u>

In an attempt to analyse the reasons why the Church adopted the Trinity, which in essence was a clear betrayal of the Scripture and the teachings of Jesus who never claimed divinity, a number of factors should be taken into consideration:

1- At that time, and unlike today, the Church had a double role. First, the Church was a constitution that provided spiritual guidance and a place of worship to people. Additionally, the Church was effectively involved in ruling the land. Religion and politics were inseparable. Anyone who dared oppose the Church was very severely punished.

The Church, being all too aware of the history of the people of Israel, knew that many prophets had come and gone and then forgotten. The Church was also aware that since the heart of the faith was the figure of Jesus Christ, then to maintain that kind of authority the Church had to keep the faith in Jesus intact. Effectively, the best insurance to guard against a forgotten Jesus figure would be the creation of a divine Jesus figure, for though a prophet may be forgotten, a god will never be. To their thinking, if Jesus was made into a god figure, the Church would never lose its commanding authority.

2- During the years that followed the death of Jesus, there was a growing conflict between the new monotheistic followers of Jesus and the multi-god Roman paganism. The Trinity doctrine, which suggests that God is One, but also three, was a convenient compromise between the two opposing doctrines.

When asked to explain how can God be one and three simultaneously, or how can God be the Father and His own son at the same time, the traditional reply of the Church is nothing other than: "Just have faith."

In other words, it does not matter that what we are telling you does not make any sense as long as you believe it. But surely, any self-contradictory concept must harbour a defect in its core. The truth is never irrational.

The word Trinity is not found in the New Testament nor was it ever preached by Jesus. It is an encroachment on the Scripture. It is philosophically inconsistent and mathematically absurd.

No sooner do we abandon the attempts to find a rational definition of the Trinity or the Father and the Son, do we come across yet another confusing title, that is the title of the Lord.

Most Christians today think of Jesus as the Lord, but in the Bible, the matter is not as clear-cut. Consider the following verses:

1- "And the Lord passed before him and proclaimed, 'The Lord, the Lord God, merciful and gracious.'" (Exodus 34:6)

It is clear from this verse that the Lord is God.

2- "Yet for us, there is only one God, the Father, of whom are all things, and we live for Him; and one Lord Jesus Christ, through whom are all things and through whom we live." (1 Corinthians 8:6)

Here the Lord is Jesus. However, the verse also asserts that only the Father is God. A clear distinction is evident in this verse between God and Jesus.

3- We also read: "The Lord is the Spirit" (2 Corinthians 3:17)

From the above verse, we realise that the Lord is any of the three. In that sense, there is not much difference between the word Lord and the word God. Thus all who say "Our Lord Jesus Christ" are in fact saying "Our God Jesus Christ." What it boils down to is that since Christian ideology perceives the Father and the Son as one, there seems little need for the terms Father and Son inside a Trinity configuration.

Some advocates will speak of the Trinity in the manner of one God in three forms. They add that there is no mystery at all since God at all times is one but the plurality is one of form. They add that a frog exists as a tadpole and also as a frog but in the end, it is the same creature.

This is fine except for one slight problem. The tadpole and the frog are not able to exist simultaneously, it is either a tadpole or a frog. If they existed simultaneously they would ipso facto be two creatures.

In the case of God and Jesus, they exist simultaneously and not one after the other as in the case of the tadpole and the frog. We have also seen how the Bible contains ample evidence of a clear distinction between Jesus and God. Jesus always acknowledged the existence of God external to himself. The following verses all make that clear distinction:

"My Father is greater than I." (John 14:28)

"Not everyone who calls me Lord will enter the Kingdom of Heaven, but only those who do what God in Heaven wants them to do." (Matthew 7:21)

"Why do you call me good? No one is good but One, that is God." (Mark 10:18)

"And this is eternal life, that they may know You, the only true God, and Jesus Christ whom You have sent." (John 17:3)

"So then after the Lord had spoken unto them, he was received up into Heaven and sat on the right hand of God." (Mark 16:19)

If Jesus and God are one, these verses and many others which clearly speak of two beings, would make very little sense. As a matter of fact, when we examine the doctrine of the Trinity, we find ourselves confronted with a concept for which common sense is not required or employed. The Scriptures testify that God is One which condemns the manufactured Trinity doctrine to being Pagan Heresy.

To conclude, the Trinity is not found in the Scriptures. It was not taught by Jesus and its advocates admit to not understanding it, still, they expect you to believe it!

Chapter 7
<u>The Atonement and the Original Sin</u>

The concepts of Atonement and Original Sin are equally precarious and not without inconsistencies. To claim that Jesus suffered and was crucified to atone for the sins of mankind is philosophically immoral. Not only does this doctrine render little sense to the merits of punishment and reward, and thus to Heaven and Hell, but more importantly, such belief assigns little need for righteousness, as long as one believes in Jesus.

It can be shown that the Atonement doctrine contradicts the Old and New Testaments:

<u>Old Testament:</u>

"Also to you O Lord, belong mercy; for You render to each one according to his <u>work</u>." (Psalms 62:12)

"And will He not render to each man according to his <u>deeds</u>?" (Proverbs 24:12)

"The <u>righteousness</u> of the righteous shall be upon himself, and the <u>wickedness</u> of the wicked shall be upon himself." (Ezekiel 18:20)

<u>New Testament:</u>

"Each of us shall give an account of himself to God." (Romans 14:12)

"Each one will receive his own reward according to his own <u>labour</u>." (1 Corinthians 3:8)

All these verses testify that faith alone is not sufficient, but that the reward is also very much dependent on one's "work", "deeds", "righteousness" and "labour." The concept of Jesus dying to take away our sins is a corruption that has been added to the Scripture. The following words from the New Testament provide evidence:

"From Zion shall come the deliverer; he shall remove wickedness from Jacob. And this is the covenant I will grant them when I take away their sins." (Romans 11:26-27)

This verse is the fulfilment of the prophecy in Isaiah:

"The ransomer of Zion and of all in Jacob who repent of their rebellion. This is the very word of the Lord. This, says the Lord, is my covenant which I make with them. My spirit which rests on you and My words which I put into your mouth shall never fail." (Isaiah 59:19-21)

By comparing the two verses we realise that the words "when I take away their sins" do not exist in Isaiah. It is clear that they have been added to the verse in Romans to justify the Atonement doctrine.

Another doctrine that was never taught by Jesus, is the concept of the Original Sin. According to this concept, all human beings carry the Original Sin of Adam upon birth. All human beings are required to atone for that sin which they never committed.

This concept, which claims that newborn babies are born with a sin, contradicts all the previous verses that assert that every man will be accountable for his own deeds and labour and that no man shall bear the sin of another. This concept also contradicts the following words of Jesus:

"Let the children come to me, and do not forbid them; for of such is the Kingdom of Heaven." (Matthew 19:14)

Since there is no sin in Heaven, and the children are of the Kingdom of Heaven, it can be said that children are free of sin.

Such concepts as the Trinity, the Atonement, and the Original Sin, all of which were never taught by Jesus but were added sometime after his death, inevitably cause disharmony when attempting to reconcile the Biblical verses with the teachings of the Church.

With regards to the Trinity for example, how can the One Indivisible God of the Old Testament suddenly become a three-in-one configuration? Has God always been three-in-one? If yes, were the previous prophets sent by God and their people kept in the dark about the true nature of God?

Why was this knowledge kept a secret even during the life of Jesus then only made known 325 years later at the Council of Nicaea?

Due to such justified questions, all with no reply other than "Just have faith", it is not surprising to find numerous Churches almost empty today.

To hold the belief in the One God and at the same time a three-in-one god is a classic case of what is defined as 'Doublethink'. In his book '1984', George Orwell defines 'Doublethink' as follows:

> "Doublethink means the power to hold two contradictory beliefs simultaneously, and accept both of them." (1984, George Orwell, p. 220)

Another case of 'Doublethink' is evident in Article VII of the thirty-nine articles of the Church of England which states:

"The Old Testament is not contrary to the New."

However, as was demonstrated, many concepts that appear in the letters of Paul contradict the Old Testament. What must be stressed here is the fact that the teachings of Jesus never contradicted the Old Testament. After all, he confessed to the following:

"Think not that I am come to destroy the law, I am not come to destroy, but to fulfil." (Matthew 5:17-18)

It is no surprise that many reputable scholars have openly opposed such concepts as the Trinity. A group among Christians known as the Unitarians insisted on the Oneness (indivisibility) of God. They emphasised the historical Jesus and avoided the use of the term 'son'. The earliest Unitarians include Irenaeus, Lucian and Arius.

Irenaeus (130-200 A. D.), who was put to death in 200 A. D., bitterly opposed Paul for injecting Pagan and Platonic philosophy into Christianity.

Lucian of Antioch (240-312 A. D.), who was also put to death for his beliefs, opposed the tendency to look for symbolic and allegorical meanings in the Scripture. He believed that Jesus was subordinate to God.

Arius (250-336), who was one of the pupils of Lucian, was one of the greatest critics of the Pauline Church.

The Unitarian school of Christianity continued to flourish to include a great host of scholars. In his Historical Account, Sir Isaac Newton (1642-1727) is quoted saying the following about the Trinity:

> "Let them make good sense of it who are able. For my part, I can make none." (Anti-Trinitarian Biographies III, A. Wallace, p. 428)

Joseph Priestly (1733-1804), who discovered oxygen, also affirmed the humanity of Jesus and opposed the Trinity. Others include the poet Milton (1608-1674), William Channing (1780-1842) and John Locke (1632-1704).

The Church was not instituted by Jesus. He never advocated a hierarchy of priests to act as mediators between God and man. Yet, the Church today teaches Christians that their salvation would be assured if they acted as the Church told them. From where did the Church derive such authority? The validity of such authority is being rejected today on a scale never been known before. One of the turning points occurred as far back as 1755 in the great Lisbon earthquake in which hundreds of Christians died in Church while celebrating the Mass. Coinciding as it did with the Age of Reason, it caused the whole concept of salvation to come under a very severe hammering (The Case against God, Gerald Priestly, p. 16).

George Harrison, known to have had a keen interest in the search for God, summed it up quite aptly with the following words:

> When you're young you get taken to church by your parents and you get pushed into religion at school. They're trying to put something into your mind. Obviously, because nobody goes to church and nobody believes in God. Why? Because they haven't interpreted the Bible as it was intended. You're taught just to have faith, you don't have to worry about it, just believe what we are telling you."(Christianity on Trial, Colin Chapman, p. 37)

With those words, George Harrison was indeed bringing to attention a very serious phenomenon. Many people who turn their backs on the Church today and are disenchanted with religion do so because of the unconvincing misinterpretations rather than their denial of God. The divinity of Jesus, a concept adopted by the Church and never taught by Jesus, also contributes greatly to turning Jews away from believing in Jesus the Messiah of whom their prophecies speak. In the Old Testament, the Messiah and King of Jews is a prophet sent to the people of Israel. He is another prophet in a sequence of many prophets. The teachings of Jesus were on the same line as those before him. But sadly the corrupted version taught by the Church today, which is more the teachings of Paul than Jesus, has made Christianity become isolated from Jewish theology.

Bearing in mind that Jesus lived all his life as a practising Jew, the Trinity, the God Incarnate, the Resurrection, the Atonement, the Original Sin and other corrupt doctrines have alienated Christianity from mainstream Judaism.

The dedicated atheist and philosopher Sir Alfred Ayer had this to say:

> Christianity is based on the notion of vicarious atonement which shocks me not only intellectually but morally. If I have a child I don't punish his brother for what he did, and that is exactly what Christianity is based upon.

Sir Ayer starts by referring to God's massacre of the Jews throughout the Old Testament then he adds:

> Here you have your deity who did all this, and then he said suddenly, 'People are behaving badly, I am going to transform myself into a human being and suffer vicariously for sins have to be atoned for by a sacrificial lamb.' So Christ is supposed to atone for the sins that other people committed. The whole thing is not only intellectually contemptible but thoroughly outrageous. (The Case against God, Gerald Priestland, p. 18)

It is not surprising, due to the poor argumentative content of such doctrines, to find Christianity constantly changing to conform to current values.

T. S. Elliot put it well when he said:

> "Christianity is always adapting itself into something which can be believed." (The Myth of God Incarnate, edited by John Hick, p. IX)

To conclude, it is quite apparent that the real Jesus of the Bible, also referred to as the Historical Jesus, is quite different from the divine figure falsely portrayed by the Church. Nowhere in the Bible is Jesus portrayed as the earthly incarnation of God. There is no evidence in the Bible to support the Atonement doctrine, nor is there any evidence that Jesus taught or believed in his own divinity.

Finally, it is apt to end this section with the words of Jesus which he directed at all those who idolised and worshipped him instead of worshipping God:

"Not everyone who calls me Lord will enter the Kingdom of Heaven, but only those who do what God in Heaven wants them to do. When Judgement Day comes many will say to me, 'Lord, Lord! In your name, we spoke God's message.' Then I will say to them, 'I never knew you, get away from me you wicked people.'" (Matthew 7:21-23)

Chapter 8
Paul, the 'Corrupter of Christianity'

It is important to note that the Resurrection is not unique to Jesus in the Bible and thus could not be taken to support the divinity of Jesus. In the following verse, we read how saints were also resurrected after they had been dead in their graves:

"And the graves were open, and many bodies of the Saints who had fallen asleep were raised, and coming out of the graves after Jesus' resurrection, they went into the holy city and appeared to many." (Matthew 27:52-53)

As for the Resurrection of Jesus, the Biblical evidence indicates that it was introduced by Paul who never saw Jesus alive. The following are the words of Paul to Timothy:

"Remember that Jesus Christ of the seed of David was raised from the dead according to my gospel." (2 Timothy 2:8)

Paul was also the first to declare Jesus as the Son of God:

"Immediately he (Paul) preached the Christ in the synagogues, that he is the Son of God." (The Acts 9:20)

Christianity of today is largely the teaching of Paul and not Jesus. The liberty with which Paul proceeded to change the teachings of Jesus is indeed alarming. The Resurrection and divinity of Jesus are among the major issues that were introduced by Paul. Other basic issues regarded as sacred in the Scriptures were discarded by Paul. Consider the following:

"God said to Abraham, 'You must agree to keep the covenant with Me, both you and your descendants in future generations. You and your descendants must agree to circumcise every male among you…

every male who is not circumcised will no longer be considered one of My people because he has not kept the covenant with Me.'" (Genesis 17:9-14)

1- Circumcision of every male was a covenant God took from Abraham and <u>all his seed</u> (Genesis 17:10). Such a covenant was decreed by God to be <u>everlasting</u> (Genesis 17:13). Nevertheless, there comes Paul to trash such covenant by declaring:

"Whether or not a man is circumcised means nothing." (1 Corinthians 7:19)

2- Later on, Paul went to the extent of openly condemning such practice:

"I, Paul, tell you that if you allow yourself to be circumcised, it means that Christ is of no use to you at all." (Galatians 5:2)

Historical accounts indicate that Jesus himself was circumcised.

It may be that Paul claimed to be an apostle and a man of God, yet some of his own words in fact portray him as a man of little integrity.

"I (Paul) robbed other Churches, taking wages from them to minister to you." (2 Corinthians 11:8)

"What I am saying now is not what the Lord would want me to say; in this manner of boasting, I am really talking like a fool." (2 Corinthians 11:17)

"For you gladly tolerate anyone who comes to you and preaches a different Jesus." (2 Corinthians 11:4)

Sadly these are some of the words of a man after whom Christianity of today is largely based. Paul argued that it is not necessary for a person to obey the law given to Moses to be a good Christian and that in fact, the only requirement for salvation is faith. If that was the case, we may indeed wonder why then did Jesus spend the best years of his life preaching what to do and what not to do in order to enter the Kingdom of Heaven? The claim that a mere belief in Jesus automatically guarantees one's place in Heaven is in contradiction to the teachings of Jesus:

"Not everyone who calls me Lord will enter the Kingdom of Heaven, but only those who do what God in Heaven wants them to do." (Matthew 7:21)

In addition, Paul claimed that his teachings were directly revealed to him by Jesus through a vision. The fact that Paul's teachings introduced various doctrines which were never taught by Jesus raises a number of important questions:

1- Was the revelation delivered by Jesus incomplete? Did it need to be completed by another after the death of Jesus?

2- Jesus lived all his life as a Jew and followed the Law given to Moses. In his words, he maintained that he had not come to change the law:

"Think not that I am come to destroy the law, I am not come to destroy, but to fulfil." (Matthew 5:17-18)

On the other hand, we find Paul preaching a number of doctrines that violate the Law given to Moses. These two conflicting situations compel us to uphold the teachings of Jesus and not those of Paul.

Due to this marked discrepancy between the divine message delivered by Jesus and the corrupt innovations introduced by Paul, we find the latter called the "Corrupter of the gospel of Jesus" by Heinz Zehrnt (The Jesus Report, Johannes Lehman, p. 126), while William Wrede calls him "The second founder of Christianity" (Ibid, p. 127).

In the Bible, we read the following accusation against Paul:

"This man (Paul) is trying to persuade people to worship God in a way that is <u>against the law</u>." (Acts 18:13)

This serious accusation cannot be ignored, bearing in mind what Jesus said:

"<u>Think not that I am come to destroy the law</u>, I am not come to destroy, but to fulfil." (Matthew 5:17-18)

As mentioned, Jesus lived all his life as a Jew, he often preached in synagogues, and early Christians were all using the synagogues. There is no evidence whatsoever in the Bible to indicate that Jesus thought of himself as the founder of a new religion. In essence, Jesus came to correct the deviation of the Jews from the law rather than instate a new law or a new religion.

The disciples preaching after Jesus' death still maintained the Jewish law. We read for example that Simon Peter while preaching after Jesus' death still called himself a Jew who followed the Jewish religion:

"I need not tell you that a <u>Jew</u> is forbidden by his <u>religion</u> to associate with one of another race." (The Acts 10:28)

Later, after Jesus' death, and when the new religion of Christianity was established and deviated from the original teachings of Jesus Christ, Paul was expelled from the synagogues as he was accused of blasphemy and pollution:

"But the Jews … raised up persecution against Paul and Barnabas, and expelled them from their region." (The Acts 13:50)

It is important to note that at that time Barnabas still travelled and preached with Paul. Later, when Paul deviated from the original gospel, the two men parted company.

The concept of Resurrection, being a new concept introduced by Paul, was immediately attacked in the synagogues:

"And they took him (Paul) to the Areopagus saying: May we know what this <u>new</u> doctrine is of which you speak?" (Acts 17:19)

The word "new" in the verse is self-indicative.

Chapter 9
Commentary on frequently quoted verses

This chapter is devoted to analysing a number of Biblical verses that are often quoted to instate the divinity of Jesus, the Trinity and also to endorse such descriptions of Jesus as 'God the Son' and God incarnate. Each of these verses will be analysed in the light of the Bible and the only references used will also be the Bible.

Verse 1: John 10:30

"I and the Father are one." (John 10:30)

This specific verse is often used by scholars in their attempt to endorse the Trinity. They argue that the words "I and the Father are one" are quite clear in confirming that the Father and the Son are one God.

It is therefore necessary to examine these words spoken by Jesus and decide what Jesus meant when he said "I and the Father are one"?

One of the rules that must be adhered to when deriving the correct interpretation of any verse in the Scripture is that the proposed interpretation must not clash or contradict other Biblical verses. If an interpretation contradicts another verse in the Scripture, then the proposed interpretation cannot be the correct one.

When we consider the possible meanings of the above words, we start with the literal meaning or in other words that Jesus and God are one in a literal sense. This would mean that Jesus and God are equal in substance and magnitude. This meaning is what the creed of the Trinity stipulates.

Immediately we find that this literal meaning clashes with at least two verses.

44

1- In the verse that comes immediately before the verse 30, we read the following:

"My Father, who has given them to me, is greater than all; no one can snatch them out of my Father's hand." (John 10:29)

The words "greater than all", which describe the Father imply that the Father is also greater than Jesus. This would clash with "I and the Father are one" if we were to take the literal meaning.

2- In defence of this apparent contradiction, some scholars stated that when Jesus said that the Father is "greater than all" he was not speaking about himself but that the Father is greater than all others (excluding himself).

However, this interpretation is refuted when we read the following words also spoken by Jesus:

" … my Father is greater than I." (John 14:28)

The parity of Jesus and God obtained from the literal meaning of "I and the Father are one" is readily dismissed by the words "my Father is greater than I".

When Jesus proclaimed "I and the Father are one," it was when he prayed for his disciples that they all may be one with the Father:

"that they all may be one, as Thou, Father, art in Me and I in Thee, that they also may be one in Us, that the world may believe that Thou hast sent Me." (John 17:21)

And so, if the words "I and the Father are one" could not have been spoken in a literal sense, in what sense were they spoken? What do they really mean?

For the correct meaning, we refer to the following:

"Make every effort to maintain the unity of the Spirit in the bond of peace." (Ephesians 4:3)

The literal meaning of John 10:30 cannot be the intended meaning. The correct meaning of "I and the Father are one" is that Jesus and God are united in spirit and purpose, just like the believers who can also be united with God in spirit and purpose. This truth is confirmed in the following verse:

"But whoever is <u>united with the Lord is one with him in spirit</u>." (1 Corinthians 6:17)

<u>Verse 2: John 14:9</u>

Jesus answered: "Don't you know me, Philip, even after I have been among you such a long time? <u>Anyone who has seen me has seen the Father</u>. How can you say, 'Show us the Father'"? (John 14:9)

The underlined words are quoted by the Trinitarians to mean that Jesus is God incarnate and God in the flesh. As will be shown, this was not what Jesus meant when he uttered those words.

1- Jesus had full knowledge of the Scripture and thus he would not say anything or make any claims that contradict the Scripture. Jesus was a devoted and practising Jew. In his own words, Jesus declared:

"Think not that I am come to destroy the law, I am not come to destroy, but to fulfil." (Matthew 5:17-18)

Jesus would have had full knowledge of the following words which God spoke to Moses:

"No man can see Me and live." (Exodus 33:20)

Jesus would not contradict the truth in Exodus 33:20 by claiming he is God incarnate and can be seen by the people.

2- Neither would Jesus contradict his own words that he spoke to the disciples:

"The Father Himself, who has sent Me, has borne witness of Me. You have neither heard His voice at any time, nor seen His form." (John 5:37)

"No man hath seen God at any time." (John 1:18, also in 1 John 4:12)

So what did Jesus really mean when he said the words "Anyone who has seen me has seen the Father"? The true meaning of these words is brought to light by reading the following words spoken by Jesus:

"I cannot do a single thing of my own initiative. Just as I hear, I judge, and my judgment is righteous because I seek, not my own will, but the will of him who sent me." (John 5:30)

"For I have not spoken of my own initiative, but the Father who sent me has himself given me a commandment about what to say and what to speak. And I know that his commandment means everlasting life. So whatever I speak, I speak just as the Father has told me." (John 12:49-50)

"Jesus, in turn, answered them and said: "What I teach is not mine, but belongs to him who sent me." (John 7:16)

The above verses all point to one truth: Jesus showed his Father through his work and teachings. Jesus did exactly what the Father wanted him to do and taught exactly what the Father wanted him to teach. Jesus did only his Father's will.

In essence, the works that Jesus did were the Father's works through him. The natural outcome would therefore be that anyone who has seen Jesus, seen his works, and heard his teachings have also seen the work and teachings of the Father.

The alternative of taking the words "Anyone who has seen me has seen the Father" literally would mean that Jesus did not only violate the truth of the Scripture (see Exodus 33:20 above), but that he also contradicted his own words in John 5:37, John 1:18 and in 1 John 4:12.

Verse 3: John 14:10-11

"Don't you believe that <u>I am in the Father, and that the Father is in me</u>? The words I say to you I do not speak on my own authority. Rather, it is the Father, living in me, who is doing his work. Believe me when I say that I am in the Father and the Father is in me; or at least believe on the evidence of the works themselves." (John 14:10-11)

The above are also verses quoted by the Trinitarian scholars to endorse the divinity of Jesus. Let us look at the phrase "in the Father" and specifically the word "in". If we take this word in a literal sense, or in other words, Jesus is inside God and God is inside Jesus, this could prove quite problematic.

If we understand the word "in" to mean "inside" we would have God and Jesus inside one another. Is the Son inside the Father or is the Father inside the Son? It cannot be both.

If the words, "I am in the Father, and that the Father is in me" in John 14:10 conclude that Jesus is God, then what about the words:

"On that day you will know that I am in my Father, and you in me, and I in you." (John 14:20)

If we follow the same logic that says that the words "I am in the Father, and that the Father is in me" mean that Jesus is God, then equally, the words "and you in me, and I in you" spoken by Jesus to the disciples would also make the disciples God.

The issue starts to get quite messy if we propose the literal meanings of the following words as well:

"that they all may be one, as Thou, Father, art in Me and I in Thee, that they also may be one in Us, that the world may believe that Thou hast sent Me." (John 17:21)

If the words "I am in the Father, and that the Father is in me" are taken literally to mean that Jesus is God, then what do we make of

48

the words "that they also may be one - in Us" in John 17:21 to mean? If the word "they" refers to all who received the ministry of Jesus, or to the disciples in particular, would the words "that they also may be one - in Us" also mean that the disciples are God since they are "in Us"? If we take the literal meaning, how can the believers be one in "Us" (in Jesus and in God)?

The correct interpretation of all those verses is that Jesus, the disciples and all believers are in union with God. None is inside the other, but all are united in spirit and purpose.

Think of a man and a woman who get married. We often say they are one, even though they are two different beings. However, they are commanded by God to become one, in union with each other. They are even described as one flesh in the Bible:

"Therefore a man will leave his father and his mother and be joined to his wife, and they will become one flesh." (Genesis 2:24)

Just like the words in John 14:10, the words "one flesh" in Genesis 2:24 are only symbolic, denoting the union of spirit and purpose.

Finally, in confirmation of the true meaning of being one with God in spirit and purpose, we read:

"But whoever is united with the Lord is one with him in spirit." (1 Corinthians 6:17)

Verse 4: John 14:19-20

"Before long, the world will not see me anymore, but you will see me. Because I live, you also will live. On that day you will realize that I am in my Father, and you are in me, and I am in you." (John 14:19-20)

The same logic can be applied to the words in John 14:19-20. The words about Jesus is in the Father, the believers in Jesus and Jesus in the believers would be quite messy if taken literally but as explained above, they speak of unity with God in spirit and purpose.

Verse 5: Colossians 1:15

"He (Jesus) is the image of the invisible God, the firstborn of all creation." (Colossians 1:15)

This is another verse used to promote the divinity of Jesus. It is suggested that the words "He is the image of the invisible God" can only be spoken about one who is one with God in nature. If that is so, what do we make of the following Biblical words:

"So God created man in His own image, in the image of God created he him; male and female created he them." (Genesis 1:27).

If being created in God's image indicates divinity, then all the human race are also gods.

Now let us look at the words which describe Jesus as the "the firstborn of all creation". The word "firstborn" indicates that Jesus was born at some stage. However, God be praised is neither born nor will ever die. The act of being born applies only to what God creates. And indeed, the words state that Jesus was firstborn "of all creation", indicating that Jesus was among the "creation" of God. What is created, born or begotten cannot be God. The same truth is derived from the following verse:

"For God so loved the world, that He gave his only begotten Son, that whosoever believeth in him should not perish, but have everlasting life." (John 3:16)

Since Jesus was "begotten", then there was a time when Jesus did not exist. Therefore Jesus is not eternal, and since God is eternal, Jesus cannot be God (The History of Christianity, a Lion Handbook, p. 164).

Verse 6: John 1:1-2

"In the beginning was the Word, and the Word was with God, and the Word was God. He was in the beginning with God." (John 1:1-2)

This is arguably the most frequently used verse to promote the divinity of Jesus and that Jesus is God. But it is also one of the most contested and incoherent verses in the New Testament for a number of reasons:

1- The word "Word" is an abstract term while God and Jesus are entities/beings. How can a 'being' be an abstract? It would make sense for example to say that Jesus was the Word of God, or that Jesus delivered the Word of God but not that God or Jesus is an abstract "Word".

2- Even though it is not stated directly in the verse, it is suggested that "the Word" is Jesus. The words continue to say that "the Word was God". From these two statements, it is proclaimed that Jesus is God.

On first impression, this may appear to be a rational interpretation. However, a closer look alerts the reader that specific words in the two verses confirm that Jesus could not have been God.

To demonstrate this matter, we first need to look at the following verses:

"Before the mountains were brought forth, or ever you had formed the earth and the world, <u>from everlasting to everlasting you are God</u>." (Psalms 90:2)

"To the King of the ages, <u>immortal</u>, invisible, the only God, be honor and glory forever and ever. Amen." (1 Timothy 1:17)

"Do you not know? Have you not heard? <u>The Lord is the everlasting God</u>, the Creator of the ends of the earth." (Isaiah 40:28)

"Praise be to the Lord, the God of Israel, <u>from everlasting to everlasting</u>." (1 Chronicles 16:36)

The words "immortal" and "everlasting" in the verses above speak of that which has no beginning and no end but has always existed and will always exist. Unlike any mortal, God has no beginning or end. God's existence is one in which time does not exist and in which no change takes place. This description captures what is meant by a timeless existence. In contrast, the word "beginning" in John 1:1-2 immediately invalidates the timeless existence. This is because a "beginning" is a point in time; a starting point, while what is eternal has no starting point.

The impact of the word "beginning" in John 1:1-2 is one and the same as the impact of the word "begotten" in John 3:16:

"For God so loved the world, that He gave his only begotten Son, that whosoever believeth in him should not perish, but have everlasting life." (John 3:16)

What was "begotten" must have been begotten at a specific point in time. In contrast, what is eternal was never "begotten".

If Jesus was "in the beginning" (John 1:1), when exactly was "the beginning" that is mentioned in John 1:1? We already established that the word "beginning" cannot be associated with God's existence because God is eternal and thus does not have a beginning. The words that offer a rational explanation of the true meaning of "the beginning" that is mentioned in John 1:1-2 are the words describing Jesus as "the firstborn of all creation" in Colossians 1:15.

Jesus being "the firstborn of all creation" means that the "beginning" mentioned in John 1:1-2 can only refer to the beginning of "all creation". Note that the word "firstborn" which speaks of Jesus also implies a "beginning"; a point in time.

Needless to say, God, the Creator of all things, existed before He created all things, while the analysis of Colossians 1:15 indicates that Jesus was "begotten" at the beginning "of all creation" because he was "firstborn".

Let us take another look at the words in John 1:1-2:

"In the beginning was the Word, and the Word was with God, and the Word was God. He was in the beginning with God." (John 1:1-2)

Now let us focus on the words "and the word was with God". The word "with" is a word that links two separate things, persons or items.

For example, we say:

- The girl was with the boy.

- The cat was with the dog.

The use of the word "with" in such sentences negates the suggestion that the girl is the boy, or that the cat is the dog.

In John 1:1, we read the words "the Word was with God". The word "with" lies between "the Word" and "God". The use of the word "with" in this position confirms that "the Word" cannot be "God" but that they are separate items. In addition, the use of the word "with" and the implication explained above becomes problematic when we read the words that follow in the verse which are "the Word was God".

On the one hand, the word "with" confirms that "the Word" and "God" are separate items, yet the words in the verse continue to say that "the Word was God".

The problem here is quite apparent. It would be like saying:

- The girl was with the boy and the girl was the boy.

or saying:

- The cat was with the dog and the cat was the dog.

This clear disharmony between the words in John 1:1 can only be a result of an error, intentional or unintentional, in the transmission of this verse. Some Trinitarian scholars saw the problem and tried a number of suggestions to remedy this apparent contradiction. Some have changed the words "the Word was God" into, "The Word was divine" and others have come up with other make-shift interpretations.

It can be shown that the only rational interpretation can be attained if we employ the literal meaning of the "Word". First, it must be noted that Jesus is not mentioned in this verse. It is only claimed that the word "Word" refers to Jesus.

What if we accept the literal meaning of the word "Word" and not a manufactured meaning? What if we accept that the "Word" does not refer to Jesus or any person but simply refers to the "Word" of God? This would indeed provide the only rational meaning.

The Word (of God) was there with God from the beginning, and the Word was God (God's Word).

Finally, it must be said that all attempts to patch up the content of John 1:1-2 do not change the fact that the words of these two verses are incoherent. The authenticity of these two verses must therefore be brought into question.

Verse 7: John 8:58

"Jesus answered, 'Very truly I tell you, before Abraham was born, I am'" (John 8:58)

This verse, and specifically the words "I am" are quoted to claim that Jesus is God. First, we need to note that the words "I am" were uttered by Jesus in a number of verses to speak about himself. In the Gospel of John, we read the following:

"I am the Bread of Life" (John 6:35)

"I am the Light of the World" (John 8:12)

"I am the Door" (John 10:9)

"I am the Good Shepherd" (John 10:11,14)

"I am the Resurrection and the Life" (John 11:25)

"I am the Way and the Truth and the Life" (John 14:6)

"I am the Vine" (John 15:1,5)

None of the above words imply that Jesus was saying he is God. However, when Jesus said the two words "I am" without additional words to follow, these two words carried great significance. So much so that when the Jews heard these two words they were infuriated and tried to stone Jesus:

"At this, they picked up stones to stone him, but Jesus hid himself, slipping away from the temple grounds." (John 8:59)

What exactly infuriated the Jews to the extent that they wanted to stone him? Why were the two words "I am" without additions of great significance to the scholars? We find the answer in Exodus:

"[13] Moses said to God, 'Suppose I go to the Israelites and say to them, the God of your fathers has sent me to you,' and they ask me, 'What is his name?' Then what shall I tell them?'

[14] God said to Moses, 'I AM who I AM. This is what you are to say to the Israelites: I AM has sent me to you.'" (Exodus 3:13-14)

The words "I AM" were used by God about Himself in Exodus 3:13-14. As a result, when the Jews heard Jesus use these words about himself they took that to mean that Jesus was claiming to be God.

The Trinitarian scholars who preach Jesus as 'God the Son' also use this verse to support their claim.

It can be shown with Biblical evidence that when Jesus uttered these words he was not claiming to be God. The evidence is in three parts:

<u>One</u>

The interpretation that when Jesus said the words "I am" he was saying that he is God would immediately clash with a host of other Biblical verses. The following are some examples:

- "<u>You, the only true God.</u>" (John 17:3)

It makes no sense for Jesus to address God telling Him that He is "<u>the only true God</u>" then at the same time claim that he is God.

- "My Father is <u>greater than I.</u>" (John 14:28)

Once again, it makes little sense for Jesus to think of himself as God yet to state that God is greater than he.

- "I ascend to my Father and your Father, to <u>my God</u> and your God." (John 20:17)

If Jesus thought he was God, would he be saying God is his God? Does God have a god?

- "<u>I do nothing on my own.</u>" (John 8:28)

Does God do nothing on His own?

<u>Two</u>

If Jesus did not mean he is God when he said the words "I am", then what did he mean? Once again, we seek the evidence from the Bible and from words uttered by Jesus:

"So Jesus said, 'When you have lifted up the Son of Man, then you will know that <u>I am he</u> and that I do nothing on my own but speak just what the Father has taught me.'" (John 8:28)

The importance of the words in 8:28 is double fold:

1- Jesus calls himself the "Son of Man". Needless to say, God is not the Son of Man.

2- Jesus used the same words "I am" in 8:28 that he spoke in 8:58. The difference is that while the words "I am" in 8:58 can be open to different interpretations, the words in 8:28 "I am he" are decisively referring to the words "Son of Man" which precede them. In other words, when Jesus said, "I am he" he meant I am the Son of Man. He was not saying I am God.

Three

It is also significant to find evidence suggesting that the translation of 8:58 may be suspect. This becomes apparent when we learn that a number of Bibles do not use the words "I am" in 8:58 altogether. The following is a selection:

"The absolute truth is that I was in existence before Abraham was ever born!" (The Living Bible)

"Believe me, said Jesus, I am who I am long before Abraham was anything." (The Message)

"Jesus said to them, 'For sure, I tell you, before Abraham was born, I was and am and always will be!'" (New Life Version)

"I tell you the truth; I am before Abraham was born." (The Voice)

"Jesus answered, 'I tell you the truth. I already was before Abraham was born.'" (Worldwide English New Testament)

Finally, it is important to note that the word "before" in 8:58, which appears in every single Bible without exception, tells us that the point Jesus was making was a time-related matter and not an identity-related matter. In other words, Jesus was referring to who existed first, Abraham or himself.

Verse 8: Matthew 2:11

"And they came into the house and saw the young child with Mary his mother; and they fell down and worshipped him." (Matthew 2:11)

The words "they fell down and worshipped him" are quoted to support the claim that Jesus was worshipped by his followers because he was God.

First

When we examine the original Greek text of this verse, we need to look at the keyword: "προσεκύνησαν".

This is the word that has been translated to "worshipped him". This is not the correct translation. The correct translation is: they honoured or prostrated. The evidence for the correct translation can be found when we examine the large number of Bibles that do not use the word "worshipped" in the translation of Matthew 2:11. The following are some examples:

Matthew 2:11 in other Bibles

"They entered the house and saw the child with Mary his mother. Falling to their knees, they honored him." (Common English Bible)

"And having come into the house they saw the little child with Mary his mother, and falling down did him homage." (Darby Translation)

"And having come into the house, they saw the Child with Mary His mother. And having fallen-down, they paid homage to Him." (Disciples Literal New Translation)

"And on entering the house they saw the child with Mary his mother. They prostrated themselves and did him homage." (New American Bible, Revised edition)

"And when they entered the house they beheld the child with Mary his mother. Falling to their knees, they paid him homage." (New Catholic Bible)

"On entering the house, they saw the child with Mary his mother; and they knelt down and paid him homage." (New Revised Standard Version, Anglicised) also (New Revised Standard Version, Anglicised, Catholic Edition)

"And having come to the house, they found the child with Mary his mother, and having fallen down they bowed to him." (Young's Literal Translation)

<u>Second</u>

Let us assume for a moment that the word "προσεκύνησαν" means "worshipped", which it does not, but we do so just for argument's sake. The essential question would be:

Can the incident mentioned in this verse about people worshipping Jesus, be taken as evidence that Jesus is God? To help with the answer, consider the following:

The people of Pharaoh worshipped him as god. Would their worship of Pharaoh be considered evidence that Pharaoh was indeed God?

Other people worshipped the sun, fire and other articles. Would such acts of worship necessarily mean that the Sun, the Fire and other items are God?

The answer to all the above is negative. The mere act of a people worshipping a person or an item does not constitute evidence that such a person or item is in fact God.

Verse 9: Matthew 14:33

The same argument used in Matthew 2:11 is used in Matthew 14:33 to make a case for Jesus being God:

"And they that were in the boat worshipped him, saying, truly thou art the Son of God." (Matthew 14:33)

Once again, the words "worshipped him" are quoted to make the case. Similar to the case of Matthew 2:11, the claim is refuted when we examine a host of other Bibles and how they translated this verse:

Matthew 14:33 in other Bibles

"But those in the ship came and did homage to him, saying, "Truly thou art God's Son." (Darby Translation)

"The disciples who were in the boat went down on their knees. They praised Jesus and they said to him, "It is true. You are really the Son of God." (Easy English Bible)

"The men in the boat bowed down in front of Jesus and said, "You are truly the Son of God." (God's Word Translation)

"The others sat there, awestruck. "You really are the Son of God!" they exclaimed." (Living Bible)

"Those who were in the boat did him homage, saying, "Truly, you are the Son of God." (New American Bible, Revised Edition)

"The men in the boat bowed down in front of *Yeshua* and said, "You are truly the Son of God." (Names of God Bible)

"Then the men in the boat bowed down in front of Jesus. They said, "You really are the Son of God." (Worldwide English New Testament)

"And those in the boat having come, did bow to him, saying, "Truly -- God's Son art thou." (Young's Literal Translation)

It is to be noted that bowing down, which is an act of respect, is not the same as the act of worshipping. People bow to Kings and Queens, but that does not make them gods.

Verse 10: Matthew 28:17

"And when they saw him, they worshipped him; but some doubted." (Matthew 28:17)

The claim, the argument and the response to Matthew 28:17 is identical to those in verses 8 and 9 above. It would therefore be sufficient here to present the translation of this verse in other Bibles:

Matthew 28:17 in other Bibles

"When they saw him, they prostrated themselves before him, although some doubted." (New Catholic Bible)

"When they saw him, they prostrated themselves before him, although some doubted." (Orthodox Jewish Bible)

"When they saw him, they bowed down to him; but some doubted." (World English Bible)

"On entering the house, they saw the child with Mary his mother; and they knelt down and paid him homage." (Darby Translation)

"When they saw him, they bowed down in front of him. But some people were not sure." (Worldwide English New Testament)

"And having seen him, they bowed to him, but some did waver." (Young's Literal Translation)

Verse 11: John 20:28

"Thomas said to him, 'My Lord and my God!'" (John 20:28)

The proponents of the Trinity claim that, more than all other verses, this verse in which Thomas calls Jesus God is the most conclusive in confirming that Jesus is God.

Reading John 20:28 in isolation may indeed lead to such a conclusion. To read this verse in the correct context we need to look at the events leading to the words spoken by Thomas.

Previously, when Jesus appeared to the disciples after the crucifixion, Thomas was not with the other disciples. The other disciples told Thomas that they had seen Jesus and that he was resurrected but Thomas replied:

"Unless I see the nail marks in his hands, put my finger in the wounds left by the nails, and put my hand into his side, I won't believe." (John 20:25)

Eight days later, Jesus reappeared to the disciples and Thomas was among them. Jesus said to Thomas:

"Put your finger here. Look at my hands. Put your hand into my side. No more disbelief. Believe!" (John 20:27)

To this, Thomas responded: "My Lord and my God!" In the original Greek text, the words read word for word: "The Lord of me and the God of me."

It is important to also note that less than two weeks previously, just before the crucifixion, Jesus was in the company of the disciples and Thomas heard Jesus pray to his heavenly Father and say:

"And this is eternal life, that they may know <u>You, the only true God,</u> and Jesus Christ whom You have sent." (John 17:3)

On the fourth day after that prayer, or on his day of resurrection, Jesus sent a special message to Thomas and the other disciples by means of Mary Magdalene:

"Jesus said to her, 'Don't touch me, for I am not yet ascended to my Father: but go to my brethren, and say to them, I ascend to my Father, and your Father; and to my God, and your God.' Mary Magdalene left and announced to the disciples, 'I've seen the Lord.' Then she told them what he said to her." (John 20:17-18)

Thomas knew from Jesus' very own words "my God, and your God" that his God was also the God of Jesus. He also knew from Jesus' words "my Father, and your Father" that his Father was the Father of Jesus, for that was exactly what Jesus instructed Mary Magdalene to tell the disciples. In addition, Thomas saw Jesus worshipping God and he heard Jesus declare that God the Father is the only true God.

It is inconceivable thus to state that after witnessing all the above evidence Thomas would inexplicably burst out calling Jesus his living, true God. Unless Thomas was a mixed-up man with muddled thoughts, how could it be possible for Thomas to hear Jesus witnessing that God the Father is the only true God and then suddenly have a change of heart and start to call Jesus his God?

Since Thomas already knew that Jesus had a God who was also Thomas' God, and since he knew that the Father of Jesus is also his Father, then it is clear that when Thomas said "My Lord and my God", he was not calling Jesus God, but was uttering those words to glorify the power of God who ordained the resurrection of Jesus Christ.

This is not any different than when we see a beautiful item, act or person and we would say, "Oh my God!" Naturally, we would not be calling the beautiful item or person God.

Verse 12: Mark 2:5

"³ Some men came, bringing to him a paralyzed man, carried by four of them. ⁴ Since they could not get him to Jesus because of the crowd, they made an opening in the roof above Jesus by digging through it and then lowered the mat the man was lying on. ⁵ When Jesus saw their faith, he said to the paralyzed man, "Son, your sins are forgiven."

⁶ Now some teachers of the law were sitting there, thinking to themselves, ⁷ "Why does this fellow talk like that? He's blaspheming! Who can forgive sins but God alone?" (Mark 2:3-7)

The words "your sins are forgiven" in Mark 2:5 spoken by Jesus to the paralyzed man are also quoted by the Trinitarians to justify that Jesus is God. They argue that:

- Only God can forgive sins.

- Jesus said to the man "Your sins are forgiven".

- Therefore, Jesus is God.

1- When we examine the words in Mark 2:5, we note that Jesus did not say to the man "I forgive your sins" but he said, "Your sins are forgiven." The difference between the two phrases is that the statement "I forgive your sins" can only mean that it was Jesus who forgave the sins. However, the words spoken by Jesus in Mark 2:5 which are "Your sins are forgiven" can also mean that the sins were forgiven by God.

2- Elsewhere in the Bible, we read that when Jesus appeared to the disciples, he told them:

"If you forgive anyone's sins, their sins are forgiven." (John 20:23)

The words in this verse say that by forgiving other people's sins, the disciples would have the sins of those people forgiven. But since only God forgives sins, would that also make the disciples God (if we follow the Trinitarian logic)?

Needless to say, this is an incorrect conclusion. The disciples are not God, nor do the words in Mark 2:5 make Jesus God. So how should we understand the words in 2:5 and also John 20:23?

It can be shown that in Mark 2:5 Jesus was telling the paralyzed man that his sins had already been forgiven by God. Jesus was simply making that known to the paralyzed man. In the same way, when the disciples were to say to any individual that his "sins are forgiven", it would also have meant that his sins had already been forgiven by God.

In Mark 2:5, Jesus was neither forgiving sins by himself, nor was Jesus reading God's mind by saying that God had forgiven the sin of the paralyzed man. All that Jesus was doing, after he sensed the faith of the paralyzed man and those with him, was proclaiming what he already knew from the Scripture about God's infinite mercy and forgiveness. Being a practising Jew, Jesus had full knowledge of the vast number of verses that proclaim God's mercy and forgiveness especially those with sincere faith. That is what Jesus was saying after acknowledging the faith of the paralyzed man and those with him. Jesus was merely reiterating the truth in the following verses:

"The Lord our God is merciful and forgiving, even though we have rebelled against him." (Daniel 9:9)

"For I will forgive their wickedness and will remember their sins no more." (Jeremiah 31:34)

"I will cleanse them from all the sin they have committed against me and will forgive all their sins of rebellion against me." (Jeremiah 33:8)

"Praise the LORD, my soul, and forget not all his benefits — who forgives all your sins and heals all your diseases." (Psalms 103:2-3)

"Who is a God like you, who pardons sin and forgives the transgression of the remnant of his inheritance? You do not stay angry forever but delight to show mercy. You will again have compassion on us: you will tread our sins underfoot and hurl all our iniquities into the depths of the sea." (Micah 7:18-19)

"I have swept away your offenses like a cloud, your sins like the morning mist. Return to me, for I have redeemed you." (Isaiah 44:22)

It was for that reason that Jesus said to the man "Your sins are forgiven." and not say "I forgive your sins".

To conclude the subject of this chapter, it has been shown how the above verses, quoted to justify that Jesus is God, have been subject to quite untenable interpretations. It has also been shown how a number of the verses used were presented in inaccurate translations. The purpose of such attempts was mainly to manufacture what serves the Trinity doctrine. It has also been shown how such references violate the true message and teachings of Jesus Christ.

It can also be shown how it is possible to combine specific verses in a manner that serves a desired doctrine or another. This can be done by stringing together a number of verses and using them out of context. The following is an example of how some verses can be combined to produce a totally false outcome:

1- In Genesis 3:2-6 the serpent tempted Eve:

"[2] The woman said to the serpent, 'We may eat fruit from the trees in the garden, [3] but God did say, 'You must not eat fruit from the tree that is in the middle of the garden, and you must not touch it, or you will die.'

[4] 'You will not certainly die,' the serpent said to the woman. [5] 'For God knows that when you eat from it your eyes will be opened, and you will be like God, knowing good and evil.'

[6] When the woman saw that the fruit of the tree was good for food and pleasing to the eye, and also desirable for gaining wisdom, she took some and ate it. She also gave some to her husband, who was with her, and he ate it."

2- In Revelations 12:9 it says that the serpent is the devil:

"[9] The great dragon was hurled down—that ancient serpent called the devil, or Satan, who leads the whole world astray. He was hurled to the earth, and his angels with him."

3- In Matthew 16:23 Jesus says to Peter, "Get behind me Satan":

" Jesus turned and said to Peter, 'Get behind me, Satan! You are a stumbling block to me; you do not have in mind the concerns of God, but merely human concerns.'"

It can be said that if we string the above three verses in such an order, we would be able to say that Peter is Satan who tempted Eve in Heaven to eat the fruit of the forbidden tree.

Naturally, this is not the case. The above was merely an example that demonstrates how it is possible to manipulate any verses to justify any desired claim or doctrine.

Chapter 10
The 'Get out of jail card'

Due to the fact that the Trinity doctrine is not found in the Bible and because it violates countless verses in the Bible, the early Trinitarians faced a torrent of criticisms centred upon the claim that Jesus is the second person in the Trinity, namely, God the Son. To justify the un-Biblical Trinity, an urgent need arose to construct an additional concept that would alleviate the criticism against the un-Biblical Trinity, offer an alternative interpretation for the numerous challenging Biblical verses and most of all, that would make the Trinity believable. Basically, a solution had to be found to explain how Jesus is called a man throughout the Bible which disqualifies him from being God.

Throughout the Bible, Jesus is portrayed in a different category than the Father. The Father is always spoken of as having no limitations. In contrast, Jesus, being a man, has various limitations. There are numerous verses that make his limitations clear. Jesus confessed that the Father is greater than him (John 14:28), that he was not omniscient (Matthew 24:36), that he did nothing on his own but always as the Father commanded him (John 8:28) and that he was not infallible (Mark 10:18) and so on.

To prop up the doctrine of the Trinity, the Trinitarians came up with the doctrine of the Double Nature of Christ. According to this doctrine, Jesus has two complete natures: one fully God and one fully man. He is simultaneously perfectly divine and perfectly human, having two complete and distinct natures at once. The doctrine of the Double Nature teaches that these *two natures* are united in one person; the God-man. In other words, Jesus is not two persons. He is one person with two natures.

Needless to say, nowhere in the Bible does Jesus claim, directly or indirectly, that he has two natures or that he is both man and God. Nevertheless, the new un-Biblical doctrine (Double Nature) was adopted to justify another un-Biblical doctrine (Trinity).

The irony does not stop there, the doctrine of the Trinity states there are three *persons* (Father, Son and Holy Spirit) in one (divine) *nature*, while the doctrine of the Double Nature reverses the order of this terminology and states that there are two *natures* in one person.

Since neither the Trinity nor the Double Nature are proclaimed in any verse, scattered verses are stringed together from which it is implied that the two doctrines are validated. In addition, the reasoning employed in the development of the Double Nature doctrine is so arbitrary that it requires very little scrutiny before the mind recoils at the propositions put forth in support of the doctrine of the two natures in Christ.

The Double Nature doctrine reduces numerous Biblical verses that are clear and straightforward into nothing other than a collection of riddles. If Jesus is fully God and fully man at the same time, yet <u>still one person</u>, then the suffering of the <u>one person</u> of Jesus was unreal, his temptation was a mere show and his prayers to God were insincere. The obvious reason for that is that God does not suffer, is not tempted and does not offer prayers to anyone.

The ultimate goal of the Trinitarians in developing the Double Nature was twofold:

1- By maintaining that Jesus had two natures but is still <u>one person</u>, it would make him the focal point for our worship.

2- Not less importantly, the adoption of the two natures of Jesus, human and God, provides a template reply to all the Biblical verses that debunk the Trinity. The following are a couple of examples that demonstrate how this doctrine is employed:

- When John 17:3 is quoted where Jesus addressed God with the words, "You, the only true God", which clearly confirms that Jesus is not God, the Trinitarians employ the Double Nature reply and say, 'It was Jesus in his human nature as a man who was addressing God'.

- When Matthew 24:36 is quoted where Jesus said that he did not know the time of the Hour, which confirms that Jesus was not Omniscient, then he cannot be God who is Omniscient. Once again, the Double Nature card is employed to say, 'It was Jesus in his human nature as a man who was not omniscient and not in his Godly nature'.

The above are only two examples, however, the same process is used to answer all such Biblical verses which provide clear evidence that Jesus is not God.

In essence, the Double Nature doctrine has become the 'Get out of jail card' for the Trinitarians. Needless to say, it must be emphasised once again that neither the Double Nature doctrine nor the Trinity doctrine are supported by the Scripture.

The articles of the Double Nature doctrine are as follows:

1- Jesus has two complete natures: one fully God and one fully man. He is simultaneously perfectly divine and perfectly human, having two complete and distinct natures at once. The *two natures* are <u>united in one person</u>.

2- Jesus was man during his earthly life. That phase came to an end when he was resurrected and was no longer man but God Himself.

When we come to the crucifixion, the Double Nature doctrine implies that it was the human nature of Jesus that died on the cross, while his divine nature lived on elsewhere. If Jesus were God, and God is immortal, Jesus could not have died. We are told to accept that Jesus does not represent the whole person. Nothing in the Bible suggests that Jesus is the name of his human nature only. If Jesus is the whole person and Jesus died, he cannot be God.

Now let us revisit some among numerous Biblical verses that turn both the Double Nature and the Trinity doctrines on their heads.

<u>Verse 1:</u>

"My <u>Father is greater than I</u>." (John 14:28)

Let us look at the keyword "I". The word "I" is a pronoun. There are various types of pronouns in the languages that we use. Let us first look at some types of pronouns that do not include the word "I".

- Relative pronouns, such as the words: whose, which, that.

- Possessive pronouns, such as the words: mine, yours, hers, his.

- Demonstrative pronouns, such as the words: this, that, those, these.

Now we come to what are called <u>personal pronouns</u>, such as the words: I, you, he, she, they.

These pronouns are called personal pronouns because <u>they refer to a person</u> or persons. A personal pronoun does not refer to an attribute or a nature of a person, but to a definite person.

The terms *(I), (me) and (myself)* always denote one person and all that comprises that one person. As an example, the significance of the word "I" when Jesus proclaimed "my Father is greater than I" (John 14:28) cannot be overstated. Jesus was stating very clearly and without any ambiguity that God is greater than <u>Jesus the person</u>. Jesus was not saying that God is greater than one of the two natures of himself.

To mould the words "My father is greater than I" in John 14:28 into what fits the Double Nature (in one person) doctrine, the promoters of this doctrine have violated basic definitions of the language we speak and specifically the definition of personal pronouns. The word "I" in "My father is greater than I" speaks of <u>one person</u> in any language.

Therefore, when Jesus declared "My father is greater than I" he was referring to himself <u>as a person</u> and not to one of his natures. Had Jesus said 'My Father is greater than one of my natures' the matter would have been different.

The above allows us to construct a case of syllogism:

<u>Premise 1:</u> The Double Nature doctrine states that the two natures of Jesus are one person.

<u>Premise 2:</u> Jesus declared that God is greater than him (the person).

<u>Conclusion:</u> God is greater than the two (claimed) natures of Jesus.

Naturally, God is greater than the nature of Jesus as the fully man, but what exactly does it mean to say that God is greater than Jesus the fully God? Does it mean that God the Father is greater than God the Son? If that is the intended meaning, it would immediately clash with the Trinity doctrine which states that God is three persons, <u>all equal.</u> That is one of the inevitable muddles that results from adopting doctrines that violate the Bible and that violate the teachings of Jesus Christ himself.

<u>Verse 2:</u>

"So then after the Lord had spoken unto them, he was received up into Heaven, and sat on the right hand of God." (Mark 16:19)

With all the verses that speak of events that happened during the life of Jesus on earth and which demonstrate that Jesus was not God, the Trinitarians have been using the 'Get out of jail card' to say that these verses relate only to Jesus the man while he was still on earth.

The situation becomes a bit tricky when we read the words in Mark 16:19. The context of this verse relates to an event that happened after the resurrection and when Jesus was no longer on earth and thus no longer a man.

If Jesus was no longer Jesus the man, but Jesus the God after his resurrection, and after he was "received up into Heaven", then how can God be sitting "on the right hand of God"?

Verse 3:

"I ascend to my Father and your Father, to <u>my God</u> and your God." (John 20:17)

When the advocates of the Double Nature doctrine are asked: if Jesus is God, then how can we explain Jesus saying "my God"? Does God have a god?

The reply once again is by using the 'Get out of jail card' to say that when Jesus uttered the words "my God", he uttered them as Jesus the fully man. This once again proves to be quite problematic. The question here is when does the Scripture say that Jesus became divine? We have 3 different versions:

1- As far as the general consensus goes, Jesus did not become the Son of God (fully God) until his resurrection:

"[32] We tell you the good news: What God promised our ancestors [33] he has fulfilled for us, their children, by <u>raising up Jesus</u>. As it is written in the second Psalm: <u>'You are my son</u>; today I have become your father.'" (Acts 13:32-33)

"[3] regarding his Son, who as to his earthly life was a descendant of David, [4] and who through the Spirit of holiness was <u>appointed the Son of God in power by his resurrection from the dead</u>: Jesus Christ our Lord." (Romans 1:3-4)

2- According to the gospel of Mark, he goes a bit further back in time. Jesus was fully human up until the point when he was baptized by John the Baptist, when he became the divine Son of God:

"⁹ At that time Jesus came from Nazareth in Galilee and was <u>baptized by John</u> in the Jordan. ¹⁰ Just as Jesus was coming up out of the water, he saw heaven being torn open and the Spirit descending on him like a dove. ¹¹ And a voice came from heaven: 'You are my Son, whom I love; with you I am well pleased.'" (Mark 1:9-11)

3- As for John, Jesus was fully God from the very beginning:

"<u>In the beginning</u> was the Word, and the Word was with God, and <u>the Word was God</u>. (John 1:1)

The importance of the above verses is that they all agree that by his resurrection, Jesus was fully God. It also means that all the time Jesus was fully man he was not God. This idea immediately clashes with the Biblical assurance that <u>God is eternally God</u> and not only from a starting point. This stumbling block cannot be resolved unless we totally reinvent the definition of fully man to incorporate a godly nature. Now let us look one more time at John 20:17:

"I ascend to my Father and your Father, to <u>my God</u> and your God." (John 20:17)

The timing of the utterance of these words is decisive. These words were uttered by Jesus after the crucifixion and <u>after his resurrection</u>. And so, whichever version we consider of the three time-related versions above, Jesus would have said that he ascends to "my God and your God" after the resurrection and after becoming fully God. How can fully God say "My God"? Once again, does God have a god?

Finally, the claim that the one person of Jesus even in multiple natures is God raises serious questions concerning the absolute ability of God. God, being perfection, does not fail in any endeavour that He undertakes. He only needs to say "be" and it is. An example of this truth is demonstrated in the following words:

"And God said, "Let there **be** light," **and there was** light." (Genesis 1:3)

To say that Jesus was God Incarnate coming down to earth to deliver mankind from sin and convert the sinners to righteous believers would lead us to doubt God's ability to execute His will. It is a fact that there are still millions of non-believers today in the world who do not believe in God nor in Jesus. Would that mean that God failed in His mission of coming down to deliver mankind from sin? Such a suggestion is inconsistent with the concept of the Omnipotent God who merely says "be" and it is.

<u>Verse 4:</u>

"One day Jesus was praying in a certain place. When he finished, one of his disciples said to him, 'Lord, teach us to pray, just as John taught his disciples.'" (Luke 11:1)

If Jesus is God, who was he praying to? When this question is asked of the Trinitarians, some reply that the prayer of Jesus was only symbolic, he was merely setting an example and teaching the disciples how to pray.

The following commentary was taken from "Our Heavenly Father Has No Equals" by Don Snedeker:

> Dr. Adam Clark, in his great zeal for the doctrine of the Two Natures, says — "Not that *he* needed anything, for in him dwelt all the fullness of the Godhead bodily; but that he might be a pattern to us." If the learned Doctor is correct, Jesus must have asked his heavenly Father for innumerable blessings which he did not need, that he might be a pattern to us. But how can we imitate such a pattern without praying for such things as *we* do not need? <u>If Jesus is God, he must have prayed to himself</u>. But of what benefit to us can such an example be? What comfort or instruction can be derived from contemplating the prayers of Jesus, if every prayer he

offered was addressed to himself, and he was so independent that he needed nothing? "Being in agony he prayed more earnestly: and his sweat was as it were great drops of blood falling down to the ground." Was all this only to set us an example? What sympathy can we feel with the sufferer, if he needed nothing he prayed for? Prayer is an expression of dependence and want. If a person who needs nothing prays, is it not mere pretence?—is it not hypocrisy?

In addition to the compelling commentary by Don Snedeker, the claim that Jesus was praying to set an example or to teach his followers how to pray comes unstuck when we read other verses where Jesus often prayed in seclusion:

"And when he had sent the multitudes away, he went up <u>on a mountain by himself to pray</u>." (Matthew 14:23)

"He often <u>withdrew into the wilderness and prayed</u>." (Luke 5:16)

"One of those days Jesus went <u>out to a mountainside to pray</u>, and spent the night praying to God." (Luke 6:12)

The obvious question is: How can Jesus be teaching the prayer or setting an example when he was "on a mountain by himself" or when he "withdrew into the wilderness"? The three verses above totally obliterate the "setting an example" excuse. As a result, other Trinitarian scholars have once again resorted to the 'Get out of jail card' of the Double Nature. They claim that when Jesus prayed, it was during his earthly life before his resurrection, in other words, it was at a time when he was still fully man.

And so, let us analyse this issue carefully:

1- Who was Jesus praying to? In his own prayer words, his prayers were addressed to God the Father.

2- According to the Trinity, Jesus is God incarnate and according to the Double Nature, Jesus had two natures but is one person who is also God. So was Jesus praying to that person whom he himself was?

3- If we follow the Double Nature doctrine, was Jesus praying to one part of his two natures, to himself, or to a part of himself? A nature cannot pray to another nature. Equally one person cannot pray to himself.

Not only does the Double Nature doctrine not resolve the inquiries related to the prayers of Jesus, it actually clouds the whole issue and exposes the frailties and inconsistencies of the Trinity doctrine.

<u>Verse 5:</u>

"For there is one God, and one Mediator between God and men, the man Christ Jesus." (1 Timothy 2:5)

This is one of the numerous verses in which Jesus is called a man. The verse also states that Jesus is the mediator between God and men. In an act of mediation, a mediator mediates between two separate parties. Therefore there are always three parties in any act of mediation, two separate parties and a mediator (go-between) who mediates between them. By definition, the mediator cannot be any of the other two parties, otherwise the mediator would be mediating between himself and a second party.

The Double Nature doctrine says that Jesus is fully God and fully man. So let us consider both of these manifestations of Jesus in the light of 1 Timothy 2:5 which states that Jesus is the mediator between God and men.

<u>Case 1: Jesus the fully God</u>

In this case, Jesus cannot be God, for then he would be mediating between himself (as God) and men. It makes little sense to say that God is mediating between Himself and men. Since mediation implies at least three parties and not two, this interpretation cannot stand unless Jesus as fully God is a different God.

Case 2: Jesus the fully man

In this case, Jesus can indeed be the mediator between God and the rest of mankind.

The conclusion of this matter is that Jesus cannot be God in any form if he is to be regarded as the mediator.

The doctrine of the Trinity also comes unstuck by the words in 1 Timothy 2:5. According to the Trinity, God is three persons in One: the Father, the Son and the Holy Spirit. All three are God. Jesus, who God the Son, is God. If we apply the words in 1 Timothy 2:5, it would mean that God (the Son) is mediating between God (the Father) and man. But isn't God the Father and God the Son One God? And since the Trinity endorses God the Father and God the Son as One God, then once again, God cannot be the mediator between Himself and man. The Trinity remains an improvised piece of jargon that even its promoters admit to not understanding by saying, 'a mystery that we do not understand'.

Verse 6:

"Now a mediator is not a mediator of one, but God is one." (Galatians 3:20)

The words "a mediator is not a mediator of one" say that mediation cannot apply to one party but implies multiple parties of at least three, two parties and a go-between mediator. As for the words "but God is one" confirm that Jesus cannot be God, for Jesus cannot be two parties, a mediator and at the same time God.

According to the Double Nature doctrine, Jesus is fully God and fully human yet still one person. Since God is One, the mediator cannot be God. Jesus cannot be the mediator and also God.

The only feasible understanding and the only reality is that Jesus was fully man and not fully God. As a man, he was indeed the mediator between God and the rest of mankind.

When the Double Nature doctrine is subjected to scrutiny, it becomes necessary to determine the meaning of a nature. A nature is merely a list of attributes or characteristics that describe an object or a person. A nature cannot do anything or act on its own. A nature is not a living entity with an independent conscience and awareness. Similarly, a nature does not die because it is not a living thing to begin with. However, Jesus died. The Bible does not say that Jesus' human nature died but simply that Jesus, the person, died.

The words of Jesus were not uttered by a nature but by a person. The acts that Jesus performed were not performed by a nature but by a person.

The Double Nature doctrine states that Jesus has two natures but is one person. The claim is that Jesus was fully man and also fully God. Doesn't that make a 4-person Trinity composed of three divine persons and one human person? To wiggle out of this tricky situation, the human Jesus is spoken of as a nature, not a human person, nor a human being. This is the word trickery that the Trinitarian teachers have inherited and just assume it is an explanation, so they never verify it or analyze it. This is because their allegiance to their creeds and their establishments is stronger than their loyalty to the Scriptures and the truth. All that they do when they are engaged in a rational discussion, which they know they cannot win, is to resort to the familiar escape clause of "It's a divine mystery".

Naturally, if we accept the truth about Jesus that is confirmed in the Scripture, that he was the Son of Man (Matthew 16:27) sent by the One true God (John 17:3) to preach the kingdom of God (Luke 4:43), all the mist would clear and all the grey clouds would disappear.

Chapter 11
Conclusion

The Biblical research conducted in this book presented a large number of decisive verses. The direct and straightforward meaning of such verses should be the only acceptable meaning if the truth is to be attained. When Jesus uttered the words that are quoted in this book, he was not uttering riddles, he was proclaiming so many truths, his words must be respected for the truth they contain without allowing any attempts to alter or manipulate their meaning.

As was demonstrated throughout this book, the historic alterations that gave rise to such doctrines as the Trinity and the Double Nature of Jesus could not have been instated without the deliberate distortion of the words and teachings of Jesus. That Christians worldwide would believe, adopt and promote such doctrines that clearly distort Jesus' own words is shocking. Sadly, the corruption went unpunished for far too long.

The various doctrines analyzed in this book, such as the Trinity, God incarnate and the Double Nature are not only clear deviations from the mission and purpose of Jesus, but are blatant insults to the Majesty of God Almighty.

For the Church to advocate doctrines that they themselves profess to not understanding, yet to expect that they would be adopted by the believers is also insulting to the intelligence of the believers.

For the Church to insist that Jesus is both God and man, they have made of Jesus a case of Dissociative Identity Disorder, the definition of which is two different natures residing in the same person.

When a false doctrine is advocated long enough its terminologies become so entrenched that it no longer seems strange to hear them. The words that define the Trinitarian doctrine have been uttered so frequently that, as absurd as they may be, they go unchallenged. This is a prime example of the old proverb, "If you repeat a lie long enough, it will become believable." The following are such examples of absurd claims that have been repeated for so long that have become incontestable:

1- According to the Double Nature doctrine, Jesus of the human nature is not part of the Trinity. However, Jesus of the godly nature is part of the Trinity. In other words, Jesus is a member of the Trinity and not a member of the Trinity. By any rational reasoning, this can only describe two persons, but no, there is only one person. Unable to justify how Jesus can be a member of the Trinity and not a member of the Trinity at the same time, the Trinitarians resort to saying that the Trinity is a "great mystery" that no one can explain or understand.

2- According to the Trinity, God exists in three persons yet He is One God. They add that those who deny the existence of the Trinity usually do so because they cannot understand it. Nevertheless, they also say that those of us who accept the Trinity doctrine don't fully understand it either. Perhaps they ought to explain how they know that the Trinity is true when they cannot explain it, understand it nor is it found in the Scriptures.

It is interesting to read the following statements:

"Theologians agree that the New Testament also does not contain an explicit doctrine of the Trinity." (Vol. 15, pg 54, Encyclopaedia of Religion).

"The Trinity is not directly and immediately the word of God." (1967, Vol. XIV, pg 304, Catholic Encyclopaedia).

3- The Trinitarians also state:

"It was the human part of Jesus that died on the cross, not the divine."

"Only Jesus' human nature died on the cross."

"When Jesus died, the human nature died, not the divine."

The question is: How can only part of one person die? The Trinitarians teach that Jesus is two natures and not two persons, yet they treat the two natures as two persons.

By teaching that the man-nature died on the cross for our sins, but the God-nature did not die on the cross for our sins, the Trinitarians have divided Jesus into two persons who do different things from each other. Jesus is not one person. If there is a Jesus who died and a Jesus who didn't die, that would be two persons.

4- It is often told that the duality of natures can be spoken of as "roles." In the role of a man Jesus did such works, and in his divine role Jesus did such works. However, a role does not indicate a person. A person can act in a role, but a role has no personal existence. Needless to say, there is no Biblical support for the notion that Jesus acted in a human role sometimes and in a divine role at other times.

5- To state that Jesus the fully God had abilities and knowledge not available to Jesus the fully man is also untenable. If Jesus had two natures in one person, then surely the knowledge known to the one person would be available to both natures. If it were not, then Jesus must have possessed a duality of mind and awareness. This duality of mind and awareness cannot exist unless there are two persons.

Knowledge resides in the mind and not in a nature, and since one person cannot have two minds, one that knew everything and another that did not know everything, the two natures doctrine has no merit unless we now want to make the irrational claim that mind and person are not correlated.

The above were some examples of the contradictions that arise when men desert the Scripture and promote man-made doctrines. The historical times and events during which such false doctrines which constitute the fabric of Christianity today were adopted are as follows:

1- First Council of Nicea (325 AD)

The doctrine of the Trinity was adopted.

2- First Council of Constantinople (381 AD)

The equality of the Holy Spirit with the Father and the Son.

3- Council of Ephesus (431 AD)

It was decided that Mary is the bearer of Christ's divine nature. Mary was to be called Theotokos, a Greek word that means "God-bearer" (the one who gave birth to God); and hence the term "Mary, mother of God".

4- Council of Chalcedon (451 AD)

The notion of a single nature in Christ was repudiated. It was declared that Jesus has two natures in one person and hypostasis. The council also affirmed the completeness of his two natures: Godhead and manhood. It goes without saying that none of the above doctrines, formulated few centuries after the death of Jesus, were ever taught by Jesus nor are they supported by Biblical reference.

It goes without saying that none of the above doctrines, formulated few centuries after the death of Jesus, were ever taught by Jesus nor are they supported in the Bible. One may wonder what Jesus in heaven feels about these deviations from his teachings.

It only remains to direct the following question to the Trinitarians who have corrupted the message of Jesus:

If you confess to not understanding the Trinity, and if you do not have Scriptural authorization for such a doctrine, for God's sake, why do you insist on selling it?

Chapter 12
Glossary

The following glossary contains key Biblical verses that are instrumental in proclaiming the truth about the One God and Jesus the man who was sent by the One Almighty God.

The Bible is not a book of puzzles, it is straightforward and offers guidance. The reader is advised to read the verses in the glossary for their face value and without adding or removing words, nor manipulating words to imply they mean something else.

<u>Glossary of Biblical verses that debunk the man-made doctrines</u>

1	Jesus proclaimed in clear words that God is the only true God. And in 1 Corinthians, it is confirmed that only the Father is God.	"And this is eternal life, that they may know <u>You, the only true God,</u> and Jesus Christ whom You have sent." (John 17:3) "Yet for us, there is only one God, the Father." (1 Corinthians 8:6)
2	Jesus proclaimed that the only One to worship and serve is God.	"You shall <u>worship the Lord your God, and Him only</u> you shall serve." (Luke 4:8)
3	Jesus was sent by God.	"I have not come on my own; <u>God sent me.</u>" (John 8:42)

4	Glory comes from and belongs to God only.	"How can you believe, when you receive glory from one another and do not seek the glory that comes from God only?" (John 5:44)
5	God is the Giver of life and is self-existent while Jesus was granted life.	"The Father is the source of life and has life in Himself, so He has granted the Son also to have life in himself." (John 5:26)
6	God is immortal, everlasting; not begotten nor firstborn.	"To the King of the ages, immortal, invisible, the only God, be honor and glory forever and ever. Amen." (1 Timothy 1:17) "Before the mountains were brought forth, or ever you had formed the earth and the world, from everlasting to everlasting you are God." (Psalms 90:2) "Do you not know? Have you not heard? The Lord is the everlasting God, the Creator of the ends of the earth." (Isaiah 40:28) "Praise be to the Lord, the God of Israel, from everlasting to everlasting." (1 Chronicles 16:36)

7	Jesus was "begotten".	"For God so loved the world, that He gave his only <u>begotten Son</u>, that whosoever believeth in him should not perish, but have everlasting life." (John 3:16)
8	Jesus was "firstborn".	"He (Jesus) is the image of the invisible God, <u>the firstborn of all creation</u>." (Colossians 1:15)
9	God is Omniscient (All-Knowing).	"If our hearts condemn us, we know that God is greater than our hearts, and <u>He knows everything</u>." (1 John 3:20)
10	Jesus does not know everything (not omniscient).	"But <u>nobody knows when that day or hour will come</u>, not the heavenly angels and <u>not the Son</u>. Only the Father knows." (Matthew 24:36)
11	God is neither man nor Son of Man.	"God is <u>not a man</u>, that He should lie; <u>neither the Son of Man</u>, that He should repent." (Numbers 23:19)
12	Jesus was a man.	"Men of Israel, hear these words: <u>Jesus of Nazareth was a man</u> attested to you by God with powerful works and wonders and signs, which God did through Him in your midst, as you yourselves know." (Acts 2:22)

13	Jesus was Son of Man.	"For the <u>Son of Man</u> shall come in the glory of his Father with his angels; and then he shall reward every man according to his works." (Matthew 16:27)
14	Jesus proclaimed his subordination to God.	"My <u>Father is greater than I</u>." (John 14:28) "No <u>messenger</u> is greater than <u>the One who sent him</u>." (John 13:16) "My Father, who has given them to me, is <u>greater than all</u>." (John 10:29)
15	Jesus confirms that his miracles are God-given by thanking God after performing them.	"Jesus looked up and said, 'Father I thank you that You have heard me, and I know that You always hear me. I say this for the benefit of the crowd standing here so that they will believe that you sent me.'" (John 11:41-42)
16	God is not tempted by the devil.	"God cannot be tempted by the devil." (James 1:13)
17	Jesus was tempted by the devil.	"And Jesus ... for forty days in the wilderness was tempted by the devil." (Luke 4:1-2)

18	No man has seen God or can withstand seeing God. In contrast, people saw Jesus and walked with him.	"No man has seen God at any time." (John 1:18) "No man shall see Me and live." (Exodus 33:20)
19	Jesus acknowledged his fallibility and that only God is infallible and perfect.	"Why do you call me good? No one is good but One, that is God." (Mark 10:18)
20	Jesus observed prayers in worship of God.	"He often withdrew into the wilderness and <u>prayed</u>." (Luke 5:16) "And when he had sent the multitudes away, he went up on a mountain by himself to <u>pray</u>." (Matthew 14:23) "And being in anguish he <u>prayed</u> more earnestly: and his sweat was as it were great drops of blood falling down to the ground." (Luke 22:44)
21	Jesus prostrated before God.	"He (Jesus) <u>fell with his face to the ground and prayed</u>." (Matthew 26:39)

22	Jesus acknowledged that it is God's will (not his) that is supreme.	"He walked away, perhaps a stone's throw, and knelt down and prayed this prayer: 'Father, if you are willing, please take away this cup of horror from me. But <u>I want Your will, not mine</u>.'" (Luke 22:41-42)
23	Jesus proclaims that he does nothing on his own authority.	"Jesus said: When you have lifted up <u>the Son of Man</u>, then you will know that I am he and that <u>I do nothing on my own authority</u>." (John 8:28) "<u>I cannot do anything by myself</u>. Whatever I hear, I judge, and my judgment is just because I do not seek my own will, but the will of the One who sent me." (John 5:30) "For <u>I have not spoken of my own initiative</u>, but the Father who sent me has himself given me a commandment about what to say and what to speak. And I know that his commandment means everlasting life. So whatever I speak, I speak just as the Father has told me." (John 12:49-50)

24	Jesus calls God the Father of all people and not only his Father.	"I ascend to <u>my Father</u> and <u>your Father</u>, to my God and your God." (John 20:17)
25	Jesus proclaims that God is his God.	"I ascend to my Father and your Father, to <u>my God</u> and your God." (John 20:17)
26	The terms "Son of God" and "children of God" as used at the time of Jesus.	"We are the <u>children of God</u>." (Romans 8:16) "You are the <u>sons of the living God</u>." (Hosea 1:10) "Blessed are the peacemakers for they shall be called <u>sons of God</u>." (Matthew 5:9) "Those who are led by God's spirit are <u>God's sons</u>." (Romans 8:14)
27	If Jesus became fully God after being raised to heaven, how can "fully God" sit on the right hand of God?	"So then after the Lord had spoken unto them, he was received up into Heaven, and <u>sat on the right hand of God</u>." (Mark 16:19)
28	If Jesus is the literal Son of God because he had no human father, should Adam also be the literal Son of God since he had no father and no mother?	"Adam the <u>Son of God</u>." (Luke 3:38)

29	If the Holy Spirit (3rd person in the Trinity) is the father of Jesus, why is God (1st person) called the Father?	"Now the birth of Jesus Christ was as follows: After his mother Mary was betrothed to Joseph, and before they came together, she was found with <u>child of the Holy Spirit</u>." (Matthew 1:18)
30	Jesus called the messenger of God in the Bible.	"No <u>messenger</u> is greater than the One who sent him." (John 13:16)
31	Jesus called the prophet of God in the Bible.	"Jesus said to them: A <u>prophet</u> is not without honour except in his hometown and in his own household." (Matthew 13:57) "I must journey today, tomorrow and the day following for it cannot be that a <u>prophet</u> should perish outside of Jerusalem." (Luke 13:33) "This is the <u>prophet</u> Jesus." (Matthew 21:11) "He who receives a <u>prophet</u> in the name of a prophet shall receive a prophet's reward. And he who receives a righteous man in the name of a righteous man shall receive a righteous man's reward." (Matthew 10:41)

32	Jesus called the servant of God in the Bible.	"Truly, I say to you, a <u>servant</u> is not greater than his Master." (John 13:16) "Behold, My <u>servant</u> whom I have chosen." (Matthew 12:18) "To you first, God having raised up His <u>servant</u> Jesus, sent him to bless you." (Acts 3:26)
33	Jesus declared that he will disown all who idolised and worshipped him instead of worshipping God.	"Not everyone who calls me Lord will enter the Kingdom of Heaven, but <u>only those who do what God in Heaven wants them to do</u>. When Judgement Day comes many will say to me, 'Lord, Lord! In your name, we spoke God's message.' Then I will say to them, 'I never knew you, get away from me you wicked people.'" (Matthew 7:21-23)

34	It is declared in unequivocal words in the Old Testament that God is One. It is also confirmed in the words of Jesus that God is One. Never is there any mention that God is three in one.	"Hear, O Israel: The Lord our God, the Lord is one." (Deuteronomy 6:4) "One of the teachers of the law came and heard them debating. Noticing that Jesus had given them a good answer, he asked him, 'Of all the commandments, which is the most important?' 'The most important one,' answered Jesus, 'is this: Hear, O Israel: The Lord our God, the Lord is one.'" (Mark 12:28-29)

After witnessing the extensive evidence presented throughout this book, the choice is whether to follow the teachings of Jesus, who was God-worshipping, or to follow the teachings of the Church, who are Jesus-worshipping?

This choice is only meaningful if one is willing to challenge one's preconceptions. God the Omniscient knows who are the ones who value the truth but have been misguided by corrupted teachings. For such a category of believers, it is hoped that this book would provide the necessary tools of verification.

Printed in Great Britain
by Amazon